John Wimber: The Way It Was

Other John Wimber titles
published by Hodder & Stoughton

The Dynamics of Spiritual Growth
Power Evangelism
Power Healing

John Wimber:
The Way It Was

Carol Wimber

HODDER &
STOUGHTON

British Library Cataloguing in Publication Data
A record for this book is available from the British Library

ISBN-10: 0 340 73539 2
ISBN-13: 9780340735398

Typeset by Avon DataSet Ltd, Bidford-on-Avon, Warks

Printed and bound in Great Britain by
Clays Ltd, St Ives plc

The paper and board used in this paperback are natural recyclable
products made from wood grown in sustainable forests.
The manufacturing processes conform to the environmental
regulations of the country of origin.

Hodder & Stoughton Ltd
A member of Hodder Headline Plc Group
338 Euston Road
London NW1 3BH
www.madaboutbooks.com

Contents

Preface

John and I had a standing joke when we would hear of a book being written about him. I would threaten to write an exposé after he died and live off the proceeds in the Bahamas – *The Real John Wimber*, *The Other Side of John Wimber*, *The Underside of John Wimber*, etc. We would laugh as we threw around different titles.

Actually we thought there were already too many books – for John and/or against John – for there to be much interest in another one. But one morning on our way home from church he spoke seriously about it for the first time ever. He had heard rumours that a biography was actually being written and he was disquieted.

'When I die, you write the book, Carol, and tell them the way it was.' At the time I protested that I couldn't write anything, much less a book, but he answered me as he had so many people all over the world, as they claimed they couldn't heal the sick, or cast out a demon or hear the voice of God: 'Of course you can.'

I promised him I would, believing he would live forever, and he was dead a few months later.

It's been about six months now since John died and four months since our first-born son, Christopher, our beautiful, beautiful boy, joined him. I didn't know what to expect and I didn't know how I would be.

I have discovered what every widow already knows, that my experience in the observation of others as they go through loss proved to be an inefficient tutor, and I was not prepared for the devastating grief – one can't be until it's staring you in the face. I somehow had the mistaken notion that it would get easier as time went on, but the reality is that it's worse, because they're just gone longer. Like when they had been gone a long time on a ministry trip and the pain of missing them would grow, not decrease.

I suppose what actually happens is that you grow used to the pain of their absence. I'll know more about it later, but now I think I'm ready to start this book.

Carol Wimber
Pentecost, 1998

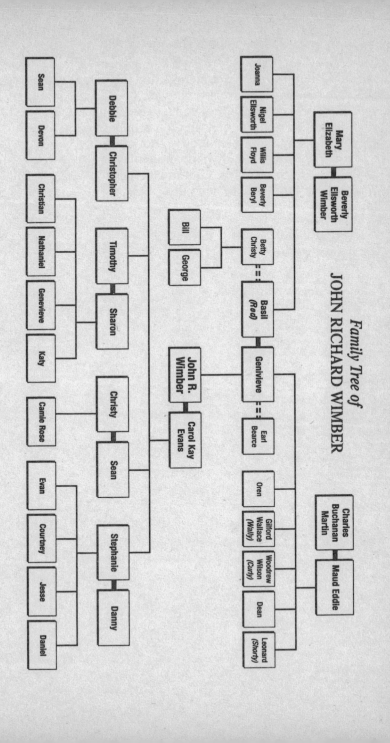

Family Tree of
JOHN RICHARD WIMBER

Early Childhood and the Family
1934–1946

The Martins

The Martins, one-time Missouri farmers, were Charles Buchanan Martin (John's grandfather), and his wife Maude Eddie Martin (John's grandmother).

Oren Martin, Gilford Wallace Martin ('Wally'), Woodrew Wilson Martin (known as 'Curly'), Dean Martin, and Leonard Martin (who was called 'Shorty') were the uncles.

Genevieve Estelyn Martin, John's mother, was the only girl in the family and the second to the youngest. The family called her 'Sissy'.

Lately, knowing I was going to write this book, I've been thinking a lot about John's rather colourful and semi-exotic family – or so they seemed to me, having been raised with just a few uncles and aunts and with my grandparents only minor players in my life.

John's family, however, was full to bursting with uncles, aunts, cousins and other kinfolk all revolving around the hub of the wheel, his grandparents, Charley and Maude. There were other family members not there but not forgotten, like Curly's first wife who was beautiful, though round (she weighed about 250 pounds), and had run off with a civilian while Curly was in the Navy; and there were always the mysterious references to 'Red' and 'the little boys' (John's absent father and his, as yet, undiscovered half-brothers).

John was raised with the Martins, his mother's family. There are reasons for this and I've heard it from both sides now – from the Wimbers as well as the Martins, though the versions of what happened vary slightly. But I'll get to that later. The point is that Genevieve, John's mother, was living back at her family home when John was born and it stayed that way.

Curly, Genevieve's brother, introduced 'Red' to her. His actual name was Basil Wimber and he was Curly's best friend. I think there was 'bad blood' (as they say in the hills of Missouri) between the Martins and the Wimbers even before Genevieve married Red. The Wimbers had kept their farm through the Great Depression of the 1920s, and the Martins lost theirs. Perhaps there was jealousy and resentment. Nevertheless, when Genevieve and Red married, it only lasted the few months until Genny came back home to the Martins. None of them ever spoke to the Wimbers again.

Now, years later, I know why and understand, but John grew up knowing almost nothing about the Wimbers. What he *did* know about his father didn't cause him to want to know any more and, if it hadn't been for Uncle Curly, we would never have met George and Bill Wimber, John's half-brothers.

We only found them recently, about a year and a half ago, through the efforts of our daughter Stephanie. John, raised apart from his half-brothers and his father's family, and only hearing vague references to the two 'boys' (as we came to think of them, though we knew they were probably just a few years younger than John), simply was not sure that the two brothers even existed; that is, until Uncle Curly came right out and said so. 'Yeah, Red married a nice little girl after he and Sissy split up, and they had two little boys. Out on leave [from the Navy], and I went to see them. They were living in Detroit then. Found her in bed, starving to death and no one caring for the little ones. So I tracked down Red and beat the hell out of him, got some groceries and took care of her and the little boys until I had to go back.' This conversation took place about thirty-three years ago and we didn't ask what 'her' name was, or what the boys' names were – I don't think we asked anything at all. We had learned over the years that any time Basil's (Red's) name came up, everybody was suddenly silent or changed the subject.

When we received the telephone call from Basil – 'Hello? Is this the home of John Richard Wimber?' – I answered in the affirmative to the man with the strong Missouri accent and he said, 'Well, honey, tell John Richard his daddy's on the phone!' Up until then what we knew about Basil Wimber was very little. We knew that John's grandfather who was Sissy's father, Charley Martin, had run Basil out of town the night John was born. We knew he had married another woman and they had two boys. We heard that he had starved that woman to the point of death. We knew that Basil came back to Kirksville and promised John a tricycle that he didn't deliver, until Uncle Curly once again beat the hell out of him (Uncle Curly's words). And the last we had heard from Basil was when he requested by mail that John, at twenty-one years of age, sign over the rights to Basil's Army Veteran benefits. John refused and bought a nice saxophone and our first car with the proceeds.

It seemed that just about everybody hated Basil. A possible exception might have been John's mother, Genevieve. She would never say anything against Basil and when the others would start to deride him, she remained silent. John asked her once why she left Basil. 'Didn't you love him?' 'Oh, I loved him,' she answered, 'but there are some things you can't live with.' Years later when we got in touch with the Wimbers, we found out from Aunt Juanita Wimber, Basil's older sister, what 'some things you can't live with' might have been. 'We loved him. He was our little brother, but we know he done wrong to Genny. And that other little girl he married, and those sweet little boys – he just didn't take care of his family. Oh, he would do anything on earth for any one of us but he didn't care about his own family. He had such a bad temper. He just drank too much. Ooh Lord, forgive him.' And she would tear up with the emotion of what had evidently been heartbreaking for her, but for us, until then, it had been merely a casual mystery.

With this being our entire knowledge of the man, when he showed up at our door (the first time when Christopher was a baby and, again, some years later) we sent him away as swiftly as we could. The last time he came, he looked like he had been in a fight, his face all scruffed up and his nose looking sore and red. Maybe Uncle Curly got to him again.

As Basil's best friend growing up, Curly apparently took on the responsibility of keeping him in line and, when that proved futile, correcting him as best he could. I don't know whose responsibility it was to keep Uncle Curly in line but, whoever it was, he failed grievously! Curly was wonderful looking, a true star. A charming, black curly-haired, blue-eyed handsome sailor, always wearing a dazzling smile that belied a nonchalant attitude toward violence. He had been in Normandy and, after he was wounded, had to have a metal plate put in his head. Every so often he would get these roaring headaches because fluid would build up around that plate. He would casually take out his pocket knife and cut his scalp open. He never did it in front of me – thinking I was too refined – but most of the family didn't get the same courtesy. I think he liked me because when he saw that we had no fence around our back yard, he stole a fence for us that very week. When we asked him where he got all that lovely fencing material, he answered, 'Don't know, musta' backed into a woodpile last night.' We said no more, and Uncle Curly built us our first fence.

When he was a young man on the farm in Kirksville, he arrived home one evening to find that a bully had taken his brother Oren's rifle away from him. Oren had contracted scarlet fever when he was a child and it had left him with a weak heart. Although he was the eldest son, the family protected him. Curly grabbed his shotgun and went tearing out of the farmhouse to the home of the offending party and caught them all sitting down to supper, all eight of them. Without a word, he fired the shotgun down the centre of the long trestle table, probably smiling all the while, and very politely asked for Oren's gun. It was quickly handed over and Curly brought it home and gave it to his brother, again, without a word.

It was the headaches, he said, that made it necessary for him to grow his own marijuana plants, although the thing I saw growing outside his trailer house was no 'plant'. It towered over that mobile home. It was as big as a tree! After John and I became Christians we tried to shame Curly into being a better citizen, but he pleaded the headaches. The last Uncle Curly story I remember was near the end of his life. He had undergone open-heart surgery at the Veterans' Hospital in Long Beach. About the third day he decided he'd had enough of that miserable place and somehow escaped out of there. He was found by the police, hitch-hiking down the highway on his way back to his mobile home and his garden with the unique tree.

We loved him, though. He was good to us. Our daughter Stephanie, who was twenty-five at the time she said it, told me that she thought Uncle Curly was awfully good looking for a seventy-year-old man – and he was. Good hearted, too.

John told me many stories of living in his grandfather's house in Kirksville, Missouri. He was born there. In fact, they were all born there – the Martin clan and the Wimber clan.

Charley had lost the Martin farm during the Great Depression in the late 1920s, and I was told that he was never the same. The Martin farm had been in the family for generations and these descendants of Scottish Highlanders didn't suffer with grace the government takeover of their farm. John told me that his grandfather Charley would just take off for months, 'riding the rails', taking John with him once, without even saying goodbye to his wife Maude. Although I never did get close to Maude – so I can't say I knew her well – I knew her well enough to understand why Charley hated goodbyes. It would have been worth his life to cross her. As I remember her, Maude had a sharp tongue and didn't mind letting us all, and anyone within hearing distance, know who she didn't approve of. 'Speakin' her mind', she called it. Being quite deaf in her later days, and much too vain to wear a hearing aid, she was under the mistaken impression that she was quietly whispering these caustic opinions to her confidante. It could be quite embarrassing when we were all together for some occasion, as she scanned the room for her victim, and proceeded in her stage whisper to describe just exactly what she thought of the poor sucker. She didn't take to just anybody, that was for sure. She didn't seem to take to me, but I don't think it was personal. She didn't care for any of the wives, her sons' wives or her grandsons' wives. She especially didn't like her daughter's husband Basil. She had nothing good to say about Earl, Genevieve's second husband and John's stepfather. I couldn't say she was vicious, or anything that strong. She just didn't approve of Earl, on general principles – the main being that he was married to her daughter. She didn't approve of Earl, but she had positively hated Basil, when Genevieve was married to him. Basil, on his second visit to us, told us that 'it was all Maude's doing', explaining why Charley ran him off, waving a shotgun, the night John was born. 'She always ruled that family; they all did her biddin.' It's true that all the other brothers seemed to admire Uncle Dean, the brother with the mettle to leave his mother Maude and run off to Panther Creek, Oregon. Asked, 'Why Oregon?' He quipped, 'Furthest away I could get from her!'

They had a strange relationship, Maude and Charley. She had been quite a beautiful woman, and still was by the time that I met her. I suspect she thought she could have done better after all, what with the loss of the farm and the way that Charley had turned out. She was a proud woman, too, and didn't appreciate it when I asked her about the photographs of Charley's American Indian grandmother. She would rather we thought the family was descended from kings, and she dismissed my curiosity with, 'Oh, everybody was Indian in those days!'

To make ends meet in those bleak times of bank failures and farm takeovers, Charley either made his own Scotch whisky and sold it, or he took a job as a 'Rum Runner'. Either way, it was the days of Prohibition in the States and it was illegal. As the old Country Western song says, 'If it wasn't for bad luck, I wouldn't have any luck at all'. Of course, he got caught and spent some time behind bars.

He was a mule-skinner, a wild horse breaker, a farmer, and the dispenser of homespun country wisdom. Anybody who has heard John speak has heard him quote his grandpa. On recommending that you stay with what God has taught you: 'Dance with who brung ya'.' Illustrating guidance by the example of the 'tender-mouthed' mule who needed only the lightest, most comfortable bit, compared to the 'hard-mouthed' mule that took a heavy, harsh bit to control it. The way a young mule is trained by 'yokin' it up with the old mule'. The recounting of all his illustrations could be a book in itself.

John loved his grandfather, perhaps more than any other person in his childhood. Charley died of a stroke in 1953, a few years before I met John. About six months before he died, a young Baptist preacher came by John's parents' house (in California at that time), where Charley was being cared for, and talked to him about Jesus. He went for it hook, line and sinker! He was marvellously converted and called each one of his grown children and John into his bedroom to tell them about Jesus. Embarrassment was the overriding emotion for most of them and they dismissed it as the ranting of a sick old man. But John couldn't forget it. Later he told me that the day Charley died, his grandpa sat straight up in bed and yelled, 'He's coming! Do you hear it? Do you hear the music? He's coming for me! Sweet Jesus! He's here! Do you see him? Oh, he's here!' And he died with his arms held out to Jesus. The rest of the family thought Charley was hallucinating, but John was shaken, and I believe the seeds of his salvation were planted in that room where his beloved grandfather died in the arms of Jesus.

The first time I met the whole Martin clan was at Gen and Earl's house on Thanksgiving the year we were married. I was used to big noisy family gatherings, having three sisters and two brothers myself, but nothing in my history prepared me for my new family. Everybody was there, grandparents, uncles, aunts, cousins, second cousins, great aunts and uncles, third cousins twice removed, and 'Whitey'. I never did figure out who he was, but he was at every family gathering they had until one year he drove away in the giant ten-year-old Cadillac, and we didn't see him again. 'Just "kinfolk" ', it was explained to me.

John introduced me around to the family members that I didn't know already, and I remember being overwhelmed for many different reasons. I was impressed by the general acceptance by everyone, of me. I came to know that the family stuck together and there was nothing they wouldn't do for each other, and I mean nothing! The men were outside, gathered around one of the uncles' new, or relatively new, pickup truck, and the women were all in the kitchen shaking their heads over an impending scenario that I was too new to appreciate. Uncle Oren was the only man except John and his two cousins, Dean and Andy Martin, who were still in the house. Uncle Oren, all dressed up in his new, still stiff overalls and his dress purple satin shirt, was sitting on the living-room couch by himself, rolling Bull Durham cigarettes – with real expertise, in my opinion. But he had this odd expression on his face, a sort of resigned disgust, as he would glance toward the window. I, in my innocence, started across the room to the window to see what was bothering him, but John caught my arm and led me away – but not before I saw all the adult Martin men and cousins, and second cousins thrice removed, gathered around a group of fighting men. Fighting Martins. The beer had been freely flowing all afternoon, and the progression from gathering around the newest truck to gathering around a free-for-all fight was traditional in that family. Everybody knew the sequence of events leading up to the Grand Finale Fist-Fight – that is, everyone but me.

The women were muttering in the kitchen, packing up their bowls and dishes from the delicious meal we'd shared, waiting for their men to finish their silliness in the front yard, so they could start back home. I was a little unnerved by the whole thing, never having seen grown men fight except in the movies; and, although most of these men wore cowboy boots and western shirts (except Uncle Oren), they didn't impress me as being cowboys. They all worked in construction, I think, except for Uncle Leonard who was a bartender, and Uncle Oren who, of course, didn't work away from the house at all. John and the cousins seemed to take it in their stride but no matter how hard I pressed John, he was unable to explain to me the reason those men were fighting. Despite this constant modelling of bad party manners, or perhaps because of it, neither John nor his younger cousins became drinkers or fighters.

Personally, I was amazed that those uncles were still all so good-looking, if this was the way they had celebrated the major holidays each year.

They were a nice-looking group, but different. Oren, the eldest, had to be at least six foot four inches tall in his stockinged feet and weighted in at only about 170 pounds. His work boots, clean and polished on this occasion, added another two or so inches and about twelve pounds. Leonard, called 'Shorty', was the youngest and not any taller than me. He made up for it, though, in his attire. Always impeccably turned out in a dark business suit, white shirt, handkerchief, a tasteful tie, matching cuff links and tie pin, wearing shoes you could see your face in, he made a statement that defied his lack of height.

John claimed that his Grandfather Martin, whom he called 'Charley', carried him around in his arms until John was so tall that his feet hung beneath Charley's knees. Possibly an exaggeration, but John was born with a turned-in foot (what they called a clubfoot), and had to wear a brace. Maybe that's what he remembered.

His mother said he learned to read when he was three years old, sitting on his grandfather's lap, reading the morning newspaper. Outside his mother's hearing, John told me that they put him in a Catholic school for third grade because he wasn't reading at all! It was that year in the Catholic school that he sang the lead solo in the cathedral boys' choir, in his beautiful high clear voice, and he made every Catholic in Peoria cry.

John's mother sometimes had less than accurate recall, but I believed her. The priests were so impressed by John that they trained him to be an altar boy, until the officials realised he wasn't Catholic! 'This little red-headed altar boy is as Protestant as Henry the Eighth!' John was broken-hearted over the whole affair. He was really looking forward to being front stage, with speaking parts every week, so his family told him that he could become a Catholic if he wanted to. Though nobody in that family went to any church, they were born with a genetic understanding that Martins were Protestant. So I think it was extremely generous of them to be willing to give John over to the Catholics. After due consideration, he declined.

John was the first grandchild. He lived right there in Kirksville with Charley and Maude, and they must have adored him. Maude had a sharp word for most people, but John said she was always kind to him. Though, if he had to choose sides between one and the other of his grandparents – like the time Charley took him along on one of his hobo trips – there was no contest. It was Charley. But he knew that Maude loved him, too.

All the Martins were good people. All the uncles, except Oren, drank too much but I don't think any of them were alcoholics. They had a reputation for always keeping their word and, most of the time that was good – with the exception of the few 'I'll make sure you'll live to regret that, Buddy' sort of exchanges.

Throughout much of John's early life in Kirksville, and later when they moved to Peoria, Illinois, they all lived together as one big happy family – uncles, aunts, grand-parents, mother, cousins. Whoever had a job supported the rest who didn't. Genevieve had a job at some big liquor factory where she worked for unbelievably small wages from dawn to dark, every day. She waited for the bus in the freezing snow every morning and waited again every night. That's why she came to California, she told me. It wasn't anything more than the mild weather. Years later when John and I had a mountain cabin, we wanted to take her along with our children up to the snow but she wasn't interested. She hated snow and cold and never intended to be in them again.

During those years in Peoria, when she and John lived with her parents and all the rest of them, she must have missed being a mother to her little boy. He called her 'Sissy', like they all did, and he called Maude 'Mommy'. It must have bothered Gen. She didn't have a good relationship with her mother; no one did, except possibly Oren, and there was some hurtful incident where Maude and Charley tried to get custody of John.

It was shortly after this, and maybe because of it, that Genevieve married Earl Bearce. He was a nice man who had a good job as head-waiter at the Crown Royal Hotel. It was a big fancy place in Peoria. Charley also worked there at one time or another, and I have in my possession a solid nickel-silver cream and sugar set from the Peoria Crown Royal Hotel to prove it.

I have come to realise that there are many different ways to acquire family treasures. Most of the family treasure from my side of the family came the usual way – from great-grandparents to grandparents to parents and then to me. My children will inherit – along with the Regina Music Box from my great-grandfather Julius Theodore Von Herrhaus, and the sterling from my great-grandmother, Mary Matilda – the solid nickel-silver cream and sugar set from the Peoria Crown Royal Hotel, by way of their great-grandfather Charley Martin.

I think big hotels were categorised right in there with banks and government agencies – hard-hearted institutions that 'owed you', at least a cream and sugar set. John told me that during the 1930s, when the banks were foreclosing on family farms, the James brothers, those famous bank robbers, became local folk heroes because they had lost their farm too, because of some government fiasco. So every time a gang rose up to rob those banks, unlike most

Americans – who were scandalised and horrified at what was going on – John's uncles and grandfather and most of rural Missouri were on the gangsters' side, rooting for 'The Gang!' Thought of them as Robin Hoods.

Don't misunderstand, these Martin men were not crooks or criminals because of the ill-gotten cream and sugar set. They were loyal Americans (Charley's father was named 'George Washington Martin', for crying out loud!) and they gladly signed up to go to war when the call came. (Except Oren, of course.) They were intelligent, hard-working, good men who loved their family, but had lost the farm. It was the defining event of their life.

Now John was different right from the start. A freckled redhead, like his natural father, he didn't care about the lost farm, except where it had hurt the rest of the family. They had a radio and he listened, in secret, to the black jazz station, whenever he could – which was never when Charley was around. 'Don't let me catch you listenin' to that —— music!' He didn't seem to mind that John's best friend was black, or that they lived in a predominantly black neighbourhood, but he put his foot down when it came to the music. So John complied and never let Charley catch him listening to the black jazz station.

John was only six or seven but he wanted a saxophone, wanted it very badly. I do not know, nor can I even imagine, how Genevieve got the money to buy John his saxophone. They have always been expensive, and she worked for a dollar a day. He saw it in the window of a music store, and it was love at first sight. I vaguely remember her telling me that she made payments for years to that music store. He was so small and the horn so heavy, that they had to place it up on a chair for him to play it. She somehow managed to get him music lessons, too. It must have taken half her pay cheque every month. And that was just the beginning of the expense of musical instruments, and years of music lessons, and all the band uniforms and much more, as John developed into the accomplished musician that he was. No wonder she was not delighted, after our conversion, when we announced to her that John was leaving the music business because we had become Christians. Callow, and confidently superior creatures (having been smart enough to get saved), though we were, Genevieve did eventually give her heart to Christ, and by her own request, John baptised his mother in our swimming pool. It took a few years for her to get ready. She was phobic about water. But Genevieve had it in her mind that to be accepted into heaven, she had to be willing to put her head under that water. We had suggested 'sprinkling' to her, as a less terrifying means of baptism, assuring her that it would get the job done as well as 'dunking', but she would have none of it. 'I'm going under, John.' And she did. We were so proud of her. It was on the level of watching a Christian martyr walk into the flames. Head held high, staring straight ahead, she stepped down into that deep water and John baptised her. This was a woman who was so phobic about water she would only take sponge baths or quick showers. In fact, when our Tim was about three, he lost his footing in a community pool and was going under, and though Genevieve was right there on the deck a few feet away, and the water only a few feet deep, she was paralysed with fear and couldn't move to help him. I had to struggle from the deep end through the water, like a nightmare in slow motion, to get to him. So, you can imagine our emotion, seeing her take a deep breath, for her, possibly her last, and go under. She lived another ten years, having settled her salvation in that great display of courage.

Knowing John all these years, I had wondered why he never seemed to lack confidence to try new things – to try and to fail and to try again until he got it right. There was a deep stability in him that always made him seem older than he was, as if the important things of life were already settled for him. I loved this quality about him. Being so emotionally at sea myself, it gave me a sense of security, feeling that he was anchored, on some deep inner level, to a safe place. He always seemed so sure of himself. A decided lack of 'fear of failure'. I've analysed it and I think the most important ingredient was the genuine enjoyment and pleasure

Genevieve took in John, from the moment of his birth to the day she died. Sometimes I would catch her watching John with this look of pure delight on her face. She thought anything he did and said was wonderful. A childhood of that kind of treatment has to do good things for your self-confidence. To her, he was perfect, even if the endeavour failed, and consequently, I think, he didn't mind failing. He would quote the statistics about Babe Ruth striking out so many times, before he ever got a home run. He didn't mind looking the fool if it was for a right reason and he wasn't very sensitive to what people thought of him. It didn't seem to shake him.

My theory is that he got from his mother, when he was still very young, all the acceptance, admiration and praise he'd need for the rest of his life.

I seem to have misplaced The Brothers. Well, you needed to know The Martins so you would understand John better. Did I tell you that they (still The Martins) moved out to California in 1946? Just like in Steinbeck's *Grapes of Wrath*, they came together as a group, in whatever vehicles they had, with all their earthly belongings packed in or packed on those vehicles. John swore that the tyres blew out every 150 miles. I don't really know how much of this is actual fact and how much is merely family myth, born of John's attempt to make me understand just how miserably poor they were back then. He told me that though they never were actually hungry, there were days that they ate nothing but oatmeal. Strangely enough, he loved oatmeal his whole life. I guess it didn't represent poverty to him. But wallpaper did. Too many old, old houses with cracked walls, camouflaged ineffectively by wallpaper. Water-stained and peeling, big, loose, ugly, purple cabbage roses. He made me see it all – the horror of wallpaper.

Wallpaper, in his world, was not used to beautify, but to camouflage and to insulate against the wet cold. I could smell the mildew myself, just hearing John describe it. Ironically, this house I moved to after John died had wallpaper on every wall, in every room but one. I've started taking the wallpaper down, and I will gladly dedicate the rest of my life to wallpaper removal in honour of John.

He asked his mother once, 'Sissy, are we poor?' I don't know what precipitated the question. It was something like the local church handing out toys to 'the poor people'. She told him no, they didn't have any money, but they were not poor. Poor was in the head, she said.

After the war, when they came to California, there was work for everyone and things were easier. And most importantly to Genevieve, the sun was always shining!

Poor little John had been plagued by constant and painful mastoid infections, and I know it was Gen's hope that the change to the warm weather would end the earaches. Not only did the ear problems end, but also he grew a foot a year for three years. John showed his talent in language skills almost immediately. He lost his Missouri twang in just three school days, with the help of a group of California boys that beat him up every afternoon. 'Ya talk funny, ya little hillbilly!' I wonder if the family noticed it, the bruises and the changing accent. To hear them all together later, you would swear they came from separate ends of the earth. Being a California girl myself, I'm grateful he took care of it before we met.

Privacy, for the first time – it must have been heaven to him. Gen and Earl, now with a good job at Standard Oil, bought their first house. A nice well-built California house, and John had his own room. His parents both worked, so he had all the time he wanted to practise his music and read and read and read. He became a voracious reader and that probably explains his large vocabulary. He even invented some words of his own, to the snickering delight of the few of his colleagues who knew there was no such word.

John was one of those enviable people who remember almost everything they read, and he had an ability to focus and concentrate on a level I know nothing about. He was so smart and I was so impressed at his intellect, though he seemed unaware of it – unaware that I was impressed, and unaware of his amazing intelligence. The first few months of our courtship, I disciplined myself to be a silent, interested listener, so John wouldn't catch on that I wasn't exactly on his level when it came to brains. I wasted my time, he told me later. It wasn't my brains or lack of them that attracted him to me. He didn't say what it was, but my guess is it was my gentle and quiet spirit.

The Wimbers

I need to get back to The Brothers and tell you what I know of the Wimbers, which isn't very much, even with Aunt Juanita Wimber's help. I did talk with Floyd, one of the Wimber uncles, and he told me some interesting things.

This is what I know so far: Beverly Ellsworth Wimber and his wife Mary Elisabeth had five children: a girl and four boys, in that order. Juanita Claire, Nigel Ellsworth, Basil Elton, Willis Floyd and Beverly Beryl. I've always found fascinating the contrast between the rather exotic name 'Juanita' and then the four English boy names. Starting out flamboyantly with 'Juanita', and then calming down enough to name the next four plain, sensible names. I want to know what changed in the time between Juanita and Nigel Ellsworth!

They were farmers also and it was only a few years ago when Grandma Mary Wimber died that the Wimber farm was sold. John and Stephanie drove past the farm when they went to Kirksville two years ago to see Aunt Juanita for the first time since John was an infant. George and Bill, The Brothers, were there too, having flown in to meet their Aunt Juanita for the very first time.

I have a few letters from Mary Wimber that she sent us after we had been married for about six years and Sean, our third son, had just been born. Someone must have told her where John and his family were. She sounded like a loving, Christian woman and I regret that we didn't follow up on the relationship. Rereading those letters now, as a Christian, I realise just how much our blessed lives are due to her prayers for us. She wrote us again after her beloved husband of fifty-four years died.

Dear Grand Darlings, O, your so sweet 3 boys. I shore wood love to see them. grandpa had hart truble and asthma. He Been Aling for a long time. Leaves B.B. [Beverly Beryl] & Grandma alone. Aunt Juanita Lives in Chicago uncle Floyd is in Washington they came for GrandPas funarl. We are So Sad & Broking up. We have 54 years Marryage Bliss. It wood Been 55 years 9 feb. This 1961. Grand Dad Said he Ready to go 54 more years if he only have his Health. Write me Carld Dear & John R. With all my Love & Best Wishes, Grandma Wimber and Uncle Beverly. Kiss the Babys for me.

That letter was in September, and this one in October of the same year.

Dear Grand Children
I have been aming to answer this notice of this Swell New Baby But you can See why. Our Husband & Grand father has been Sick for 4 years But only in Bead for 12 Days he was so kind and Pasion and sweet up to the end he had Hart and asthma then he tuck old Puples Pemouni he Was So offell sick We loved him So much. And now Life is a Very Sad Thing With out him. He said the Baby Picture was a Sweeter. Looks like the Bozarth Side of the house. That his Mother Side But they are So Sweet as they can Bee. Carld You are a Sweeter. May God Bless you and Keep you With all my Love Best Wishes Grandma and Uncle B.B. Write me Carld When you Can.

Those letters from the grandmother John never knew read like poetry to me now. This uneducated, kind woman loved her husband and reached out to us, her family that got away. Except for the spelling, I could have written that heart-breaking letter myself a few months ago when John died. For us it would have been forty-two years of marital bliss. I only knew Mary Wimber through her letters to me but I'm richer because of her and I look forward to seeing her on that great Day.

Apparently, Basil (pronounced 'bay-sil' like the herb), was the 'black sheep' of an otherwise fine family. Floyd called us once, wanting to come by and meet us while they were in California, but we discouraged him from doing so, thinking if Basil was as bad as he obviously was, chances were the rest of the family wouldn't be much better. Floyd pleaded with us not to judge the whole family by Basil's life, but we were young and satisfied with our life the way it was. Earl Bearce, John's stepfather, was our children's grandpa and we didn't want to hurt Genevieve and Earl by developing a relationship with the Wimbers. I'm sorry now. I wish they could have known John.

Beverly Beryl Wimber was crippled on one side, the result of infantile paralysis, meningitis and mumps all at the same time. Floyd Wimber said that although there was nothing deficient in his mind, back then there was not much tolerance for a crippled boy and he never had a job off the farm. He was taught at home and never married or even had a girlfriend. I've seen photographs of him and he was a nice-looking boy, so it's very sad. He stayed on at the farm after his father, then his mother, died, when Aunt Juanita Wimber came to care for him and tend to the farm. After Beverly Beryl died, she sold the farm.

Nigel Ellsworth Wimber, the eldest boy, had a job trucking a load of corn from Iowa to Missouri. He stopped to get some sleep, sadly choosing a viaduct to lie down on. Apparently, when the train came through, it sucked him down onto the train and he died. He was engaged to be married and he was only twenty-six. It was 1936. That's sad. Also, you may be interested to know he had one blue eye and one brown eye!

Floyd Wimber, though a few years younger than John's father, Basil, had the responsibility of getting Basil to do his allotted work there on the farm. It couldn't have been easy because Basil hated farming. In fact, Floyd told me that he only ploughed one row across the field, left the plough where the row ended and kept walking until he got to Arizona. He was fourteen at the time of his departure and Arizona suited him so well that he won the Golden Gloves State of Arizona Award when he was seventeen. That's boxing, I believe. It ought to be outlawed. (But that's just my opinion. John never thought so and he hated to watch a boxing match on television when I was around.)

When I talked to Floyd this morning, I said to him, 'Floyd, you knew the Martins as well as anybody. What kind of people were they?' He paused a while before he answered. 'Egotistical.'

Our daughter Stephanie found Aunt Juanita Wimber when she decided to try to find John's two half-brothers for him, before he died. He had survived the cancer and the stroke a year later, but we didn't know how long 'his luck would hold', so to speak. When she told Juanita who she was, Juanita sobbed. Aunt Juanita had also been totally transformed twenty or thirty years ago by the love of Jesus, and she had been praying for her nephews 'John Richard and her other two little boys', all these years. She didn't know where they were now, she hadn't seen them since the funeral of their mother, Betty Christi, who had died of cancer in Detroit where she and Basil and the little boys lived. So what Curly thought was starvation was actually cancer. Billy was five and Georgey was three then. She didn't remember Basil being at the funeral at all and couldn't remember where he was, she said. We found out later that he was in jail for statutory rape at the time and she may have known that and just not had the heart to say it to us. The Court of Detroit, Michigan gave custody to the maternal grandfather Christi and he gave them up for adoption to a childless couple he knew. Basil petitioned the court for custody, but was turned down on the grounds of extreme neglect and abandonment.

Juanita didn't know of this, of course. All she knew was that she had talked with her two little nephews at the funeral and asked them if they would like to come and live on the farm with Grandpa and Grandma Wimber and ride the ponies. They did want to, but by the time she had gone back to Missouri to prepare everything for them and get the money to bring them home, they had been adopted and their names changed. All adoption laws back then were strict, but the State of Michigan especially was known for its unbreakable adoption laws.

She couldn't talk about it even fifty-three years later without crying. When our daughter Stephanie called her and explained to her that we were trying to find John's half-brothers, she said, 'Oh, Stephanie honey, I just know Jesus has kept me alive all these years just to pray for my boys. I just can't go home until I know they're all right.' She was in her middle eighties by then and declining physically. She wanted to know all about 'John Richard' and if he'd had a good life and if his people had been good to him and had he been happy. And she cried. I hadn't realised what our decision to stay away from that side of the family had cost some of them until then. I'm sorry and I'll be able to tell her so one day.

Juanita, a widow since her fifties, had no children of her own and so it meant everything to her to find all her nephews. She knew where John was because she and a Wimber 'in-law' had seen him teaching on a Christian television station, and she also knew from Floyd and Basil that we didn't really want any relationship with the Wimbers. But they watched him, and were so proud of him, and they honoured our wishes.

It was Stephanie who wouldn't honour our wishes and started probing around, digging up information about the Wimbers. Soon, she had talked to Floyd and he was sending her photographs of the family and one of Betty Christi, Basil's second wife, and the little boys. She called Aunt Juanita herself and got the whole thing going before John knew anything about it. When he did find out what she was up to, he was actually quite happy about it. On his way through Detroit, more than once he had gone to the City Hall with the hope of gathering information that could get him in touch with his brothers. It had come to nothing, of course, because their names had been changed. We contacted a People

Finder agency but, because of the adoption laws, they didn't get very far, though we did get an address in Michigan having to do with Children's Probate and they agreed to give us unidentifying information. All we really found out was that John did have two brothers and what their ages were, which we already knew from Aunt Juanita and Uncle Floyd. It was all rather disappointing and, as the time went by, a certain desperation to find them developed in all of us. We prayed constantly and one day God brought the right people into our life to accomplish it. Just then the State of Michigan changed their adoption laws and sent us all sorts of information, some of it shocking, and it made us wonder how we could make a relationship with these brothers, or if they would even want a relationship with John when and if we found them, since the only connection was their mutual father, Basil. It was at that time that we were told where Basil was when his wife died and why he was there. He was only twenty-five or twenty-six at the time.

Steve Schultz of 'Seekers of the Lost', a Vineyard man from Seattle, heard that John was trying to locate his brothers, and he took on the job out of the goodness of his heart. Stephanie sent him all the information she had gathered and he took it from there. It wasn't long at all until we received the call from Steve that he had located Bill and George. He gave us their phone numbers and said that Bill would call us that night, and he did! It was all so exciting for us. We had started the process two and a half years before and at last we had found them! I shouldn't have been surprised when George answered our call with some hesitation. They had not known they had an older brother, and any memories they had of their father, Basil, were all bad. But good-hearted men that they are, they gave us a better chance than we had given the Wimbers, and John and I and Stephanie flew to Minneapolis to meet them. George flew down from Ohio and joined us and it was wonderful. John's brothers are fine men and we loved them at once. Later on in the year the three brothers and Stephanie (because she was responsible for initiating the whole thing) flew to

Kirksville to meet their Aunt Juanita for the first time. Aunt Juanita had 'her boys' all together at last. They drove past the Wimber farm and she showed them all the Wimber gravestones in the old cemetery. Bill asked her where her gravesite would be and she answered, laughing, 'What does it matter? There'll be no one to cry at my grave!' 'I'll cry, Aunt Juanita,' Bill answered softly, but John overheard him and it made him cry. Bill was there, true to his word, when they buried Juanita early this year.

Before I finish with John's family, I need to tell you what Juanita told us about John's birth and the trouble with the Martins. Apparently, Basil had come back from Arizona temporarily and met Genevieve Martin through Curly and she was swept off her feet. She dropped her boyfriend of long standing and went off with Basil Wimber. The Martins wouldn't let them get married, so the Wimbers took them over the state line where a seventeen-year-old boy and girl could get married without parental permission. It becomes a little fuzzy at this point but I got the impression that John was born seven months later.

Probably for the reasons that Juanita had mentioned – his terrible temper and the drinking – Genevieve was living at home again with her family when John was born on 25 February 1934. Basil tried to get in to see her, but was stopped by Charley Martin, Genevieve's father, brandishing a shotgun, which he would have gladly used on Basil. A 'Go on, make my day' kind of situation. Whatever happened must have been quite serious, because Charley spent more time in jail because of it. Basil left town frightened, and the Martins wouldn't talk to the Wimbers from that point on. Juanita told us that Beverly and Mary Wimber pleaded with them to let them see their grandchild, but they wouldn't allow it. That's all I know about it.

One interesting thing, though, before we leave the subject. Genevieve once told me that she had decided to name her baby 'Roger', but when the nurse who was filling out the forms asked the child's name, before Gen could answer, 'Roger', the attending physician interrupted her and declared, 'The boy's name is John Richard'! I think it amazing that Gen let it go at that, although I'm glad she did. Roger Wimber?

These are the people that he came from.

This was the cradle of eminence for him.

This beautiful child, this sweet little red-headed boy with the wonderful face that changed hardly at all over a lifetime.

This responsible, good boy, whom they all could count on.

This little cowboy who honestly believed that he was Tom Mix, from the western movies, and wouldn't answer to any name but 'Tom' for over a year.

This little boy who loved music, but hated wallpaper his entire life.

This talented child who was almost the first non-Catholic altar boy in Peoria.

This handsome, extraordinary child, who I can see now in the face of his grandson Daniel.

This was John.

2

Career, Marriage, Children
1946–1963

I've been looking through old school papers of John's and I can see how the move to California was very good for him. For three years in a row he never missed a day. I also found his report card for first grade (1940) and second grade (1942) and nothing from 1941 at all except a drawing of a cowboy he did on an Rx paper from Collin's Clinic. That must have been the year he had the surgery on his ear because of the mastoid infections. His mother had told me that he was very ill for a long time, but I hadn't realised he'd missed a whole year of school.

Another discovery I made; every report card he got was marked 'Talks too much, needs improvement!!' Those people obviously didn't recognise giftedness when they heard it.

Other than excellent marks for communication skills, there wasn't anything that seemed unusual to me except one recurring comment by his teachers: 'Gives up too easily'. Gives up too easily? Could this be the same John Wimber that wouldn't quit no matter what obstacles were put in his path? Even before he was a Christian, he seemed to me to have tremendous endurance and staying power. For instance, in the late 1950s and early 1960s, during the great music famine for all the serious jazz musicians, when Elvis was king, unlike most of his fellow musicians who gave up and went to teaching or sold insurance or bought music stores, John converted to rock and roll. (Prostituted his talent, in the opinion of his friends.) And a darn good rock and roll musician he was! But he didn't 'give up'. He had a wife and family by then and I was proud of him that he would work anywhere he could to take care of us.

In fact, I've never known him to give up on anything that was worthwhile. We all watched him during his last years after whatever natural strength he had was long spent, and he just kept going and going. I asked him once, at the peak of his declining health, how he could keep it up. He ruefully grinned, 'I guess I'm like the Timex watch. I can take a lickin' and keep on tickin'.' Well, he became famous around here, at least for his patient endurance, defying that early life pronouncement about him. I could have written it on his gravestone: 'He never gave up.'

If a musician were chronicling his school achievements, he would have understanding and insight that I don't have. To me it just looks like a stack of certificates and awards for musical stuff. School bands, orchestra, dance bands, lead clarinet, I Division, III Division, big gold stickers with blue ribbons attached, combos, musicals, etc. All music stuff. It was his life then. He did find time to play football and get his letter in baseball and later in golf. But his one and only true love was music. It always had been.

John had a parakeet named Sue-Bill because he didn't know if it was a boy bird or a girl bird. But whatever the gender, John and Sue-Bill shared a mutual love of music, and Sue-Bill would follow John around the house squawking his or her little head off until John would get out his clarinet. It's possible he or she had aspirations for the big time and knew it would never happen without practice. Sue-Bill would wait impatiently on his shoulder, jumping up and down the whole time while he put the instrument together, and once done, he or she would leap up on the clarinet and peck John on the mouth until he would start to play, whereupon he or she would dance and hop up and down the length of it. If he paused, the bird would hop frantically up to his lips and give him a sound peck on the nose until he got going again.

I thought you needed to know about Sue-Bill. He also

had a dog named Lady, who wasn't much of a personality in comparison to the bird.

Looking through his report cards again, I see that he got chastised in 1940 for talking too much, and they still hadn't been able to shut him up by 1946. I don't know that anything changed in 1947, 1948 or 1949. I just don't have those report cards. I suspect he was still talking too much in 1953 when he graduated from high school.

He went on to Orange Coast City College and Fullerton City College, still successfully pursuing his music and winning awards, and playing a little golf.

Musicians, to make extra money on weekends, would play for high school proms, or private parties, or bar mitzvahs and weddings and that sort of thing. In fact, I met John because he was in the band that played for my Senior Prom.

But long before that fateful event, John got his first paying job playing in a burlesque house called the 'Dixie Castle'. He was fifteen years old! I don't know how they could hire a fifteen-year-old boy, even though he looked older than he was. It smells of Uncle Curly or Uncle Leonard (the bartender) to me.

In May of 1955, when John came over in the big white steamer to Avalon on Catalina Island with the band to play for my Senior Prom, he was hoping to get a job with one of the famous Big Bands in the near future. Until then he worked weekends with this semi-good dance band and waited for the big break. He had good reason to expect this, having won the very prestigious 1955 Best Composer and Arranger at the Light House All Stars Jazz Festival. In the meantime, John was working at a bank, what the musicians called a 'day gig', and playing on weekends. He was studying privately with Jimmy Guifrey, a well-respected jazz musician, and writing and arranging better and better.

His big break did come one day about seven months later, and the band that he was hoping to join did ask him. But when he explained to me, his new bride of two weeks, how long he would be on the road, I was not at all understanding and suggested with much heartfelt emotion that perhaps we had made a dreadful mistake in getting married after all . . .

I think it was one of Woody Herman's Herd's, but I'm not sure. I forgot about it right away, but I'll bet he didn't though he never let me know. Now, I wish I had let him go. I hate the thought that I stopped him from doing something he would have enjoyed so much. He went on working at the miserable day gig until we moved out of the area. This is making me sad; I'll go on to something happier.

In May of 1955, I was seventeen years old and John was twenty-one. And he was beautiful. Those of you who only know him looking like Pooh Bear or Santa Claus, need to know that he was voted 'Best Build' of 1953 in Anaheim Union High School, a very large school with a huge student body! I was voted 'Best Figure' in Avalon High School, but there were only about twenty students and half of those were boys, so big deal. But not so with John. This was a legitimate poll of the student body and they voted John Wimber the best body in that whole school! The Student 'Body' of the year. So there!

He was a nice boy, too, and stable, emotionally. He didn't seem to go through those wild, crazy teenage years when most parents decide the best course to take would be to put the wretched adolescent in the deep freeze until he's twenty-one. I have talked to John's cousin and asked him what John was like as a teenager. 'Pretty much like he is now. He was always good to us and I never saw him lose his temper, but once.' That is what I keep hearing. He was a well-behaved, considerate child with a strong sense of responsibility, and he became a well-behaved, considerate teenager with a strong sense of responsibility, and grew up to be a well-behaved, considerate adult with a strong sense of responsibility.

And he was the most practical person I have ever known. Mere emotion couldn't persuade him – there had to be sound reasons attached to the proposition or he remained un-moved. He didn't make decisions emotionally. He would wait until he had all the information he could gather, then make the decision. Most people who worked with him over the years have heard him say, 'If you need an answer now, before God makes it clear to me, then the answer is no.'

That may sound boring to you, but it was life-saving to me. His stability was the life raft that kept me afloat until I met Jesus, and he took over that job.

An unusual combination really: the musical talent, without the 'prima donna' attitude, and I believe John made possible the prominent place the worship leaders have in the Vineyard, by just being who he was. He couldn't be moved by the worship leader's need to express himself through the music. 'It isn't about you, it's about Jesus, and your only job is to lead the people to him,' he would say. Displays of artistic temperament and endeavour left him cold. When the worship leader would go off into an introspective indulgence of musical meandering, he commented, 'I suppose to them, it's fraught with meaning, but I'm not impressed!'

He was the ultimate pragmatic artist, and because he was such a fine musician himself, he couldn't be fooled or intimidated by anyone's great talent. He fought to keep it simple, and I think he did a pretty good job.

'What good is it ultimately, if we produce worship songs that only the experienced musician can play? What will the little churches do?' He hated 'elitism' in whatever form it took, spiritual, as well as musical, and he also understood that it takes legitimate acumen and craftsmanship to write simply. He especially loved the guys who put aside what they had the ability to produce, and chose, instead, to write simple love songs to Jesus that anyone could sing or play on the guitar.

John was a professional musician, and it always fascinated me how he heard music before he was a Christian. He was totally unaware of the lyrics, but completely aware of the key it was written in, the chord changes and if any instrument was flat or sharp. Or what instruments were being used. Very unromantic about music. He never got emotional about music and never cried over a love song until it was a love song to Jesus. He couldn't stand 'background music'. 'You don't understand, Carol, it's not in the background to me. I can't not listen. I hear every single note whether I want to or not', he would patiently try to explain to me. So we only had music on when he actually wanted to listen to it, and never when he was working at something else.

So, though we fell madly in love at first sight, we didn't have 'our song.' We had 'our' restaurant, and 'our' favourite film, and 'our' private jokes, but no song, until after we were Christians. And then it wasn't our song at all – it was our song to Jesus. 'Sweet Perfume', 'God of All Comfort', 'Strangers Here', 'Praise Song', 'Together', 'Worthy is the Lamb', were all songs we wrote together. Only in that sense were those 'our songs'.

Please don't hear that music was less to him. It wasn't, it was more. It was what he did; it was his career and hope for his future, as well as his identity. He was a fine and accomplished musician. And in the music world, his future was pretty much secured. He had put together some very good show bands and had contracts for as long as he wanted in Las Vegas. He was one of the best arrangers around, and he had just recently, more or less accidentally, put together The Righteous Brothers and he wrote all their first arrangements. Bobby Hatfield was the younger brother of John's good friend in school, Carl Hatfield, and somehow John put Bobby and Bill Medley together and got them their first job as The Righteous Brothers at The Black Derby in Orange County where John was working. At the time, it was just a fun interlude until something more in his line came long. But wouldn't you know it, after all the years of hard work in show bands and jazz bands, the ultimate rock and roll group, The Righteous Brothers, become a hit, along with John's arrangements!

So that's where he was in his career in 1963, the year we became Christians. But back to May of 1955, when I first saw him.

I saw him for about four hours before I met him, because he was on the stage playing the tenor saxophone with the dance band, and I was merely one of the nondescript senior girls whirling around the dance floor. When I first saw John,

I was sure I had seen him before – he was the most familiar looking person I had ever laid eyes upon. 'Haven't we met someplace before?' I almost blurted out. I couldn't stop staring at him and I was becoming a little embarrassed in front of my date, and tried to cover it with, 'That sax player looks like someone I've known all my life'. After the dance was over, and I had been introduced to John, he turned to his best friend, Dick Heying, and told him, 'I'm going to marry that little chick.' That was me, the little chick. That's how we talked back in 1955.

I went down to the pier the following morning to see the big white steamer leave and waved goodbye to John, mouthing over the steamer blast, 'I'll write you'. He thought, or said he thought, though I find it hard to believe, that I was saying; 'I love you!' If there is such a thing as 'love at first sight', I had it, but I never would have said it.

John was captain of the band in high school and I used to tease him by telling our children that he was the guy with the tall fur hat and baton that pranced along leaning backwards. When they would ask how we met, he got me back by telling them, 'Oh yeah, I first saw your mom at the dance, peering at me out of the potted palms, and when I went to make a phone call and saw inscribed in the phone booth, "for a good time, call Carol", I knew it was love.' That's what he told our children! He stuck to his story, too, no matter how I would scream, 'John!! That's a terrible thing to say!! They are going to believe you!!' As the years went by, I didn't bother to deny the absurd story, I just gave him the look. For all I know, our children might believe it. If you say a thing enough times, it almost becomes truth, right? He was a terrible tease, and the greater the reaction, the more pleasure he got from it.

I graduated from high school in June. I had my eighteenth birthday in November and we were married in December. John would be twenty-two the following February and I had been eighteen for one month.

Knowing nothing, really, about one another, except that he was a great musician and I was a great artist, we still felt confident that our love would carry us through. I remember that, about the third day of our honeymoon, we ran out of things to talk about and there were long periods of silence. To strengthen his attraction to me, I had memorised a bunch of facts about jazz that made me appear quite knowledgeable to him and he was real impressed, I know, for about a day and a half. So we cut our honeymoon short and went home and visited his family. I didn't know these people and I was a little shy by nature, but he couldn't pass up this opportunity to tease me.

'Ma, ya wouldn't believe it! I take this little girl up to this fancy hotel and the next thing you know, there she is, nekid as a jay bird! Never so shocked in all my life! What do ya think, Ma, should I keep 'er?' That was John's sense of humour. I know I am a different person than I would have been because of it.

Which of you that knew John well enough to talk to him on the phone to set up a meeting time with him hasn't heard, 'OK then, two o'clock at the restaurant. How will I know you?' He never tired of that one. Over the years his friends developed a list of quick come-backs: 'I'll be wearing my red clown nose'; 'I'll be the only naked guy in cowboy boots'; 'I'll wear a boutonniere in my ear', and so on.

Everyone liked John. He was just that kind of person. What I thought was a unique experience to me, that sense of having known him before, was a common reaction of many people, maybe most people. It happened all the time. He'd be in an airport and a stranger would come up to him as if they'd known him all their life and begin telling him their troubles or joys or whatever. Our daughter has the same thing he had, that 'never met a stranger' thing, except the other way around for those two, they never looked like a stranger to anyone who ever saw them.

John, even before he became a Christian, was a good, honourable man. I know he had his flaws, but for the life of me I can't think of a one right now. That's part of the problem of writing, after they've died, about someone you loved. You can't remember the bad stuff. And I've tried hard. He used to give me a look when I would be theorising about some theological issue, that was meant to convey, 'Carol, you don't know what you're talking about, don't bother me with this tripe'. It would hurt my feelings that he didn't take my viewpoint seriously but I felt obligated to carry on my effort to enlighten him, so consequently, I got my feelings hurt fairly often over the forty-two years. Someone took a snapshot of John and me in one of these discussions and he has the 'look' on his face! I framed it and have it out in my family room along with all the happy loving photos of us, just to remind me that he wasn't perfect. He wasn't perfect, was he? I can't remember and there is no use asking his children or grandchildren or friends or church. They all think he was perfect, too.

I'm going to introduce you to our four children right here all at once, even before we are married. Christopher Earl, our first. Timothy Charles, close behind him. A three-year rest and then Sean Richard and Stephanie Lynn. From just these amazing four, we have extracted eleven grandchildren already, seven boys and four girls, and they aren't even through yet!

I need to tell you about our children. I know that even if no one else reads this book, they will, and how will I explain their lack of presence? It's certainly not that they are less important to John than Uncle Curly who gets so much space here in this book, but I'm a little self-conscious about talking about my own children. Perhaps a little like showing home movies. But they are John's children too, and the most important people in his life, so I'll talk about them.

Christopher was always a trendsetter, a leader. Whatever he was into, soon we all were. Like his dad, he loved people around him all the time. He organised large groups of friends to go to Flo's, a diner out in dairy country twenty-five miles away, just because he got a kick out of the farm atmosphere (that means flies and manure smell). It wasn't just the cuisine – the Number 3 Special: ham and eggs with biscuits and gravy. He was musical – played bass in his many bands he put together, and he could draw better than I, who fancied myself an artist. One semester he took a gourmet-cooking class and amazed us all when he cooked for us that night and served us a gorgeous stuffed totally de-boned chicken. He had a great sense of humour; he loved his life and seemed to be aware even at an early age that his life was unusually filled with grace.

My children were at their full height by fourteen, which in Chris's case was six foot two. He would take up the cause of the weak: protector of the geek and the nerd from bullies and other natural predators. He loved little children and never went anywhere without his own, once he had them. As a baby he loved flowers, especially the blooms in Genevieve's garden, and he would pull off all her prize-winning begonias and happily present them to her. He was non-violent by conviction and that was good because one had the impression of power under control – just barely. He was buzzing with nervous energy and his personality filled the room even when he was silent. He was a wonderful-looking young man with his long musician-style hair – red hair that he complained about his whole childhood, and then fell in love with and married a red-headed girl who looked like a twin to his sister. Debby, his wife, provided the spontaneous joy that was running out in our bloodline. She is a walking party and has somehow been trapped into doing Thanksgiving for my entire family this year – all fifty-five of us, including second cousins and guests (though we are a bit much for most potential guests and they politely decline the invitation). Two years ago we had, in the family, two members of rival gangs, though a divorce changed that by the following year. Debby is a wonderful woman and I can't imagine any other person on earth putting up with Christopher's weird ways. When they were first married, Chris took her home to the house he had bought for her from his grandfather, Earl, who was moving back to Missouri to be with his brothers and sisters. Well, Earl liked Debby so well he put off the move and lived there with the newly-weds for about six months! God bless them both, they never complained. And there was only one bathroom!

Tim was brilliant and still is, of course. He also knows everything about all things and if ever I need to know anything from astronomy to quantum physics, I ask Tim. He can build a car, and he just designed and built an extra-ordinary garden rose-arbour with a six-foot radius that is the envy of all my friends. As a child he was a delight, so sweet and affectionate and funny. Tim had something to say and he would say it all day long. He would say out loud everything he was thinking, and at night after he was tucked in the bunk bed that he shared with Christopher, he would go over all the events of his day, out loud. We thought it was darling: 'I got up and dressed in my blue shirt and then I ate my breakfast and I brushed my teeth and I played . . .' – but it drove Chris to the verge of hysteria. 'Make him stop!' Make him stop!' When we told Timmy to stop talking, he claimed he was praying. If so, he prayed more than any other five-year-old that I've ever heard of did. He prayed without ceasing. He tended to be a little stubborn at times, and he and John got into it once over corn, which Tim came to hate. He only mildly disliked it before the power encounter with his dad. He was about three years old that year, and John was about three and a half that day.

John: 'Timmy, you are going to eat that corn! You are not going to throw away good food!'

Timmy: 'I hate corn! I can't eat corn! Corn is bad! I will throw away the corn!'

A half-hour later, this is still going on, but Timmy is weakening and finally capitulates and eats the dreaded corn, but not without the final word. 'When I grow up big I will come back and break your house down!'

He must have forgiven his father somewhere along the road to adulthood because he only and always blessed our house (and still does).

Sean just reminded me that at the hospital before John's heart surgery, John overheard us making plans to eat lunch at the dingy little diner across the street, and as a last request, made us promise to go to the Summit House (a lovely restaurant) instead, where Tim ate the whole bowl of creamed corn, the first corn that had passed his lips in thirty-six years! The healing process has now begun over what will forever be remembered in our family as The Corn Incident.

Sharon, Tim's lovely graceful wife, guileless and loving, is a brunette with flawless olive skin, and she has added some pigment to our family. John and I were delighted when our first grandchild, Christian, was born, with his daddy's face and his mother's olive skin. It isn't all Sharon's doing though, John's great-grandmother was a Pawnee Indian, and it comes out in one child of every generation. No kidding.

Sean was as silent as Tim was talkative and he stayed that way. Where Christopher was able to get the whole room spinning to the point of frenzy, Sean is restful to be around. Like a strong redwood, the colour of his hair. (The colour of all their hair, really.) If I was stranded on a desert island and could choose one person to help me survive, it would be Sean. He can fix anything. He scored in the top 3 per cent in the nation in Abstract Problem Solving. If you need to get 'A' to point 'B' and there is no way, Sean can find a way. If you need to move this very large armoire through a very small doorway, Sean is your man. He understands the ins and outs of air-conditioning and car-engines and electricity and gas lines. I once asked him to make a little glass-doored cupboard to hang on the wall, though he had never done woodwork. He delivered a perfectly balanced, beautiful piece of furniture without ever looking at a pattern or a plan. I know I could say to him, 'Sean, would you please build me a rocket ship to take me to the moon?' and he would come up with it and it would get me there. He married the little girl down the street, Christy Mantilla, and fulfilled a prophetic dream that he had when he was fourteen and Christy was seven. He dreamed that he went through the hedge to Mantilla's house wearing a tuxedo and Chuck was there, too, in a tux. The pastor was waiting and he realised he was getting married to one of Chuck's daughters! I just read this part to Sean and he commented, 'It could have been a warning.' (Just Sean's sense of humour.) Christy has trained Daniel, aged two and a half, to address her as 'Beautiful Aunt Christy', and she is. 'Bootiful.' Looks like a renaissance angel but plays soccer as aggressively as the devil.

The great love of his life is his daughter, Camiline Rose, whom he produced single-handedly – to hear him tell it. When she was born they handed her to Sean and he said, 'MY baby!' – emphasis on 'MY'. They go out alone every Saturday morning and she has biscuits and gravy. On more than one occasion I have been with them when a stranger would comment to Sean, 'That is a very beautiful child, you know.' Believe me, he knows.

Stephanie had a dream about her dad the night before last and the next morning she was telling me about it. It had been a happy kind of dream where he was asking her if she needs a little honey for her bread, and putting money in her pocket, like he did so often. I asked her if he was young again like he always is in my dreams and she said no, he was not as young as in the other dreams she's had of him. His hair was getting too long and he was a little heavy and, in fact, she was thinking in her dream, 'Oh, I wish he wouldn't wear that crocheted Christmas sweater. The arms are too short and it always makes him look twice as big as he is.' At this point, I interrupted her and asked what sweater she was referring to, because John has never had a crocheted Christmas sweater. She answered, 'Oh, you know, that green heavy knit with the red stripe going through it.' No, I didn't know of any sweater like that. Then she gasped, laughing. 'I can't believe it! That's the sweater on my teddy bear!' That is a key to Stephanie's relationship with her father.

John was so proud of his daughter and with good reason, I think. She looks the most like him. Stephanie has been a delight to us her whole life. She was born in that enchanted span of time as we were being drawn to Christ and God used that pregnancy to ensure that we would stick to our intention of staying married.

The prevailing psychology thirty-five years ago was that a baby is a blank slate and the only difference in so-called male or female behaviour is modelling and moulding. I knew that wasn't true the first week that little baby girl was born. She was so totally different in every way from the boys. As soon as she could walk, she was carrying a purse and she changed her dresses five or six times a day. The poor plasterer that was plastering a long wall just the other side of our fence was held captive by Stephanie all day long, as she would toddle out to the fence carrying her purse over her arm and talking unceasingly as he worked. I was standing at the kitchen sink, listening and watching her as she went on and on talking to the back of this man, moving along the fence as he progressed along the wall. I saw him stop, lay down his trowel, slowly turn around with a smile on his face and his head cocked to the side. His hands were on his hips as he looked down at this little girl in playful exasperation, 'Are you a woman?' he asked her.

Her brothers loved her and she loved them but she was always good, in her opinion, and they were often bad. One evening I was concerned that 'the baby girl' might be upset because the boys were being disciplined over some crime or misdemeanour. I need not have worried because when I looked over at her, she was continuing to eat her dinner with a happy little smile on her face. She hates it when I tell that story.

Stephanie – how can I describe her? She has that special, star-like quality that her father had. Every day of her life she has been a blessing to us. I know she would hate this, too, but it's true. She is like the woman in Proverbs. Ask her husband. Ask her four boys. Ask her friends. Ask her relatives. Ask me. Don't ask her brothers. And she is beautiful, too. What can I say? God did her for us.

Danny, her husband and the father of four of my precious grandsons, won her hand in marriage by reminding her father that God had given him a longed-for saxophone, not because he deserved it but just because God loved him. This, after John, with narrowed eyes, asked Danny just why he thought he deserved to marry his daughter. Danny has one of those amazing memory systems where he can remember everything that ever happened to him all the way back to the womb. He remembered John's story of years before, casually shared in a kinship group, of being sent a saxophone from a friend back east after mentioning to the Lord that he missed his sax sometimes, and what a tender display of love that was to him. He surely didn't need it, and he couldn't even play it any more. It wasn't for any spiritual reason, like 'the Lord's work'; it was just because God loved John. So Danny finally cornered John in the living-room after waiting every night for a week to talk to him, only to be outwitted, as John went to bed earlier and earlier each night as he sensed Danny coming in to ask for Stephanie's hand. 'It's just because he loves me, John. God is giving her to me, just because he loves me. Like that saxophone he gave you.' John cried and gave Danny permission to marry his beloved daughter. Stephanie and I came out from where we were hiding and made bacon and eggs, at John's request, to celebrate.

May I borrow from King David words to describe her? 'She is like the light of morning at sunrise on a cloudless morning, like the brightness after rain that brings the grass from the earth.'

John loved all his girls, his stunningly gorgeous daughters-in-law (that was the only kind he had) as well as his cherished daughter. It was his pleasure and their delight when Easter came around and he would pass out the $100 bills for Easter dresses. Sharon told me once that when she and Tim were first married, she had a difficult time adjusting to John's generosity, but after a while, she decided to just relax and enjoy it.

When a particularly hot summer hit us here in Yorba Linda, John had air-conditioning put in all our children's houses. 'Those girls can't take this kind of heat, Carol.' He would get a pained look on his face if he saw that they were driving a car that he judged as unsafe, and he would work it out somehow to change the situation.

Now when we were young and without money, we drove a car that would only turn left, and we lived through the long hot summers by sitting out under the sprinklers reading wet magazines. When I reminded him of that, he came back with, 'Carol, that is precisely why I am doing this!'

He didn't spoil his kids. They never expected these kinds of things and never asked us for anything. John simply couldn't enjoy his own life without sharing with the ones he loved.

Before his heart surgery, he made me write a list. Christopher was to have his ring; Tim, his watch; Sean, his golf clubs; and Stephanie was to have her car painted and the dents taken out. I am very ashamed to admit that I didn't carry through on Stephanie's car. When John first brought up the subject, I had objected on the grounds that it would be insulting to Danny, Stephanie's husband; but when John checked with Danny, he thought it was a swell idea and maybe she would even take better care of her car. Really, she couldn't be blamed for the bashed-in right front door where Jesse, their five-year-old, had done his Ninja-flying-karate-kick.

Danny, who is riding John's horse along the 'generosity trail', got Stephanie's bug-ugly Suburban completely over-hauled and repainted and it looks like new. Not one scratch or dent. Yet. Jesse restrains himself now that he is seven and whenever the urge to kick the car overtakes him, he confines his attentions to the tyre.

That's our family.

We were married in Riverside, California on 23 December 1995 in the home of a Baptist clergyman. Although I was raised Catholic and would have felt more at home in a Catholic church, I knew John would never go through what it required in those days for a non-Catholic to marry a Catholic. So John being nothing, and me a lapsed Catholic, as sort of middle ground we chose the Baptist. At least it wasn't in the Baptist church. That would have been a more serious breach of Catholicism, in my mind. Truthfully, if he had been a Hindu, I would have married him any way and anywhere he wanted, I was so in love with him.

Being the sophisticated realists that we fancied ourselves, we were aware that marriage in 1955 was a pretty risky business. After all, we already knew many couples who had separated so, in an effort to guard against great disappointment should the marriage fail, our idea was to get quietly married and then, if it didn't work out, quietly divorced. Our thinking was, if we make a big splashy statement by doing a church wedding with all the wedding gifts, guests and folderol, then everybody will notice if we divorce later. Plus, I would feel obligated to return all the gifts. It's amazing how an eighteen-year-old reasons. But as it was, we had to tell my mother and John's parents and though we had our plain little wedding service with just two friends for witnesses, three of my sisters heard of our secret little service and were incensed at the whole idea and came anyhow. They, too, were Catholic and I'm sure it was hard on them, but they asked for it. I'm grateful to our friends, Dick and Lynn Heying, for bringing a camera, or we would have no account of that fateful day.

We stayed in the honeymoon suite at The Riverside Inn and were gloriously happy though we did run out of things to talk about after a few days and decided to go home early, which I've already related to you.

The night we got married, we prayed, which is interesting because we were both rather godless, irreligious people. I think it was John's idea, so I obediently started praying, 'Dear Jesus, we don't know what marriage is all about, so will you help us please?', and John prayed to 'God in Heaven' to make our lives worth something.

We knelt down beside that big four-poster honeymoon bed, with hands pressed together Catholic style (not fingers folded over like the Protestants, even though a Baptist had married us). In retrospect, I think it was sort of sweet, and maybe God did, too.

There was something about John that made me feel everything was going to be all right now. Maybe everyone in love feels that way, but I don't think so. I had many boyfriends before John, and I never felt anything was going to be all right now, or ever. When asked, 'Why?' by the boy-friend I was breaking up with, I answered, 'With John, I am the way I want to be, the way I am supposed to be.'

Did I mention that I had been, from as early as I can remember, seriously depressed? I didn't? Well, neither did I mention it to John. In 1955, no one thought of 'depression' as a condition that could be treated, and actually it's only in retrospect I realise that I was not a normal teenager. It's not normal to have a suicide plan ready in case life doesn't work out. By the time there was more known about it, it was too late for me because Jesus had already healed me.

'Melancholia' was what they called it in my grandmother's day, and she finally rowed out in her little boat and drowned herself. (She could hardly have chosen a worse time. My older sister, the first child, had just been born, and I can't imagine how my poor mother coped with that, and at a time when every new mother needs her own mother.)

My father had also attempted suicide and so it was perfectly natural that I was mildly suicidal. I say mildly, because I didn't try very hard too often or for any good reasons. It was more just an overall dismal outlook on life. It didn't seem worth all the trouble to live it. I'm sure there were some outside influences that contributed to the depression, but lots of people live through hell and aren't depressed. But I had been seriously depressed and the scars on my wrists should have been a clue, but this oblivious young man, John, didn't have any idea what he had married.

This is John's story and here I am talking about me, but that's the whole point of what I'm trying to say. He somehow made me know that good things were going to happen in our future. He didn't talk about it much, but it was in everything he said and did, an optimism that was based on more than illusions, and a confidence in me, that made me believe that I could do whatever needed to be done, and be whatever I was meant to be. He just assumed certain good things as if life were that simple.

'Well, we can get married next month. I've got a job that

pays enough for us to live on,' was his proposal of marriage to me.

I had planned on being dead that next month, though he didn't know it of course. But I cancelled my plans immediately and went with his.

'We can start our family now if you want, I got a raise!' Family? Children? I had never, ever thought about having children. We hadn't discussed children that I could remember, but it sounded like a plan to me, so why not? I realised it would mean that I would have to give up Plan No. 1: 'If Trouble Comes My Way (Suicide)', but it seemed worth going along with.

Again and again, over the years, I've heard men testify to that same thing that John did to them. That holy assumption. Lance Pittluck tells of when he first went to the east coast to plant a church and things weren't going well. Not even a kinship group yet and he was feeling pretty discouraged when John came to see him. They were walking around the block and John was telling him how to help all the new churches that would be started, and how to give counsel to the young pastors who would need help, and how the function of a bishop facilitates growth, and he went on like that for hours and Lance realised that it would be like that. He believed it would happen just that way, and it did.

I don't mean any 'rah-rah', pumping-you-up kind of talk; I mean the assumption that you will do what needs to be done and not give up, and the confidence in you, that you are able to accomplish the task, whatever it takes.

He wasn't very sensitive, in the way of an awareness of what others were feeling or thinking, and I think that was good. He didn't struggle with fears about his own ability or the ability of others, and part of what made him a powerful leader was his ignorance of any other perspective. He wasn't even aware of the fears most of us have about ourselves, and we were glad to give up our thoughts on the subject, in exchange for his, anyhow.

At the risk of being 'corny', the easiest way to say it is: 'He believed in me. He believed in you.' Though not particularly sensitive, it was always clear to him what a person was for and what were their gifts and strengths, and once he told us, we tended to see ourselves the way he saw us.

What he was lacking many times was the insight to see the flaws, the weaknesses in a person, especially someone he loved. My emotional problems were an uncharted ocean to him and that was just as well, because he was never fully aware of the black fog that regularly threatened to engulf me.

'If Mama ain't happy, ain't nobody happy,' was another of Charley's sayings, and though I did my best to keep my problems to myself, that is impossible as we all know, and I regularly made him, if not miserable, at least very uncomfortable.

I'm seeing this all now from the viewpoint of a sixty-year-old Christian woman who's been around the block a few times. When it was all happening, I would have blamed it on John's lack of sensitivity and his self-centredness. But I know the truth now and I know I was a time bomb with the time running out.

Three little kids: four, three, and a newborn. John working all day and most of the night, too tired to even realise I was fading away. After our third son was born, I went into a severe depression and couldn't sleep or eat for days on end. If he noticed or not, I don't remember. We were all stuffed in a little one-bedroom apartment in Las Vegas because of his job, and our newborn baby had diarrhoea so I had to stay awake and feed him one half-ounce of 7 Up every half hour so that he wouldn't dehydrate.

John, when he was tired, merely went in and laid his weary head down on his pillow and slept the sleep of the innocent. I, on the other hand, being a more complicated package, the more desperately I needed sleep, the more hopeless and unrealisable it became.

Poor John couldn't understand what was wrong with me. 'Listen, honey, just go to bed and get some sleep. I'll take care of the baby. Don't worry, you just need to rest.' I knew a snowball in hell had a better chance of survival than I did of going to sleep, but I somehow lived through that whole horrible time and eventually did sleep again.

But something bad had happened to my fragile hope for normality. The black cloak of despair dropped on me and with it the hellish understanding that no one really loved anyone else. It was all just need and selfish possessiveness, and when the stresses of life came, I and everyone else would look out for Number One.

Now, that is not a good philosophy of life to go on with, and I spent the next few months destroying our marriage and making life hideously painful for John.

This is hard for me to write and possibly unnecessary, but John's instructions to me were: 'Tell them the way it was,' I don't think it would be fair of me to be so open about everyone else in his family, and then paint myself nicer than I was. I hate the kind of person I was, and one of my biggest fears was that my boys might marry someone like I was.

Years ago I was introduced to a very strange but interesting man, who was still, even after conversion, a little odd. His life had been a self-induced nightmare before he met Jesus and he had undergone some sort of breakdown and left his professorship at the university and now lived on the streets, helping other street people. The shoes he wore were two or three sizes too big and it didn't bother him a bit. He still carried his briefcase with his name monogrammed on the corner, Charles Smith, Ph.D. He was introduced to me as 'Brother Charles' and I was very interested in his story. Curious about what had brought him to Christ, I asked him, 'Brother Charles, what caused you to get saved?' He answered me with a most profound truth, 'Necessity, my dear.' Well, that's my story, too.

John's told you about his Las Vegas experience where he heard the inner voice of God for the first time. He was there on a ten- or twelve-week contract, and both of us having given up on our marriage, it was our plan for him to file for a quickie divorce while he was there. In 1962, the divorce laws were more stringent and there were only a few places you could get a six-week divorce, Las Vegas being one of them, and it seemed a wasteful shame for us to pass up this convenient opportunity.

So that's what he was doing in Las Vegas without his family. I have described the state of mind I was in at that time and I can only imagine what he was going through. I think he was drinking too much. I know I was.

Just about the time John was starting out to the desert on the outskirts of town late one night, I was at home with the three little boys, four and a half, three and a half, and five and a half months, all asleep but me, and an idea came into my head: 'I've completely ruined our lives and have hurt the very people that I claimed to love. I must be in the hands of the devil, if there is a devil. And if there is a devil (and my actions certainly support that possibility), then there is probably a God, too, and if he is really God, he can help me and I need help!' Then I prayed, most sincerely, 'Jesus, help me!!'

He did. I hadn't even finished my prayer when the dark fog lifted off me and I could see clearly for the first time in my life. I called the club in Las Vegas and left a message for John to call me when he came back.

Meanwhile, back at the ranch, John was out in the desert contemplating the star-studded desert sky and an idea came to him also: 'Who made this sky, this moon, these stars? Did they just happen? Could there be anything in the God theory? Maybe there's Somebody up there. Somebody that cares?'

So he prayed, looking up at the sky, talking out loud, 'Hey! If You're up there, if Anybody's up there, could you give me a little help here?' He said he was aware of putting everything on the line in that moment: either there was a God who would hear and act, or he had just done a very stupid thing in talking to the sky.

He went back to town and was given my message to call me, which he did, and I asked him to forgive me and to come and get me and the kids. He drove all night, looking up at the sky often, with the new awareness that everything in life had changed.

* * *

Here we are on the brink of salvation, and I haven't even talked about what a great father John was to our three wonderful little boys and our daughter.

Christopher Earl was born about a year and a half after we married and he had red hair just like John! We were absolutely delighted with him, and when his brother Timothy Charles was born fourteen and a half months later we were in awe that we had produced these little wonders and amazed that he, too, had red hair like his father. We thought they were enough, but then Sean Richard was born, adding to our great pleasure and not complete surprise when he, too, had red hair like his father. Stephanie Lynn was born fifteen months after Sean and we were completely aston-ished that we could have a girl, but not surprised at all that she had red hair like her father.

We had this baby grand piano, the same one our daughter has now, that was our very first purchase as newly-weds, before a refrigerator or television or sofa or anything. We borrowed from family everything else we needed, or went without, but we saved our money for the essential things, like a baby grand piano.

I can still see him at that piano, working against a deadline to finish his arrangements. Pencil in his mouth, playing something and then writing it down, and the boys climbing all over him. It never bothered him. He would stop once in a while with one child on his lap and the others on each side and say, 'Let's lay down some blues, boys!', and they would all start pounding on the piano, each of them sure the good sounds were coming from their little hands.

He was the involved father, before it became the normal way to do a family. Since we had our children in sets, two babies at once, John would take the oldest one and give him his bath and get him ready for bed while I was tending the new one. He could do anything I could do and sometimes he did it better, naturally having a better disposition than me. He wasn't the helpless father, not knowing how to change a diaper or burp a baby. In fact, most nights before he would leave for work, I would have to wipe the baby spit up off the shoulder of his dress suit.

Because he worked at nights, he could be with the children in the day time, and we would go to parks and on other outings that ordinarily we might avoid because of the weekend crowds. He was wonderful with those little people and played with them all the time. He chased them all over the house, blaring his baritone saxophone, a very scary sound, and they would scream with delight and fear. Much delight, and just a little fear.

He left for work at 8.30 in the evening and returned home at 2.00 in the morning. Sean, still taking a night-time feeding, would wake up and struggle to his feet in his baby bed, every night about five minutes before John drove into the driveway, and wait. As soon as he would hear the car, he would call out, 'Da? Da? Da? Da?' until John came and lifted him out of his bed and rocked him to sleep with his night-time bottle.

Since John didn't get home until 2.00 in the morning, I wouldn't let the children near his bedroom door until about 10.30, but then they could run in and he was at their mercy and they at his.

Many of the musicians drove sports cars, but John drove a station wagon with a baby car-bed in the back.

Do you get the picture?

As the years went by, John couldn't remember how he had been with the children. He was afraid he had failed them somehow, because he wasn't into athletic things. But I told him many times that he gave his children the greatest gift a father can give. Love, integrity, honesty and respect are worth a lot more than teaching a kid to throw a ball well.

Besides that, he did teach them to throw a ball. It was the children who weren't interested in football or baseball. They wanted motorcycles.

That is something you should know about John. He had a hard time remembering any of the things in his life that he did right. Something must have been missing. He would have almost no recall of good and kind actions and words that he spoke. The only way he could record it in his memory was for me to say it all back to him. That way he would remember my words, and that is the way he recalled it later: he would remember what I had told him. Sometimes he would get the parts mixed up, and tell the story with him taking my experience and me his.

Not too long before he died he became troubled trying to remember if he had been generous with our daughter Stephanie when she was planning her wedding. 'Did we get her the wedding gown she wanted? I'm so afraid I didn't give her what I should have.' He had given her specific instructions to pick out the dress she wanted and not to worry about price, but he couldn't remember that, or many of the kind, generous things he did or the kind generous person he was.

In fact, John was the most generous man I have ever known. I had to be careful not to let him know if I admired some piece of jewellery or clothing. For me to want it was for him to buy it for me. I didn't dare show interest in any item in the store window, if I wasn't prepared to take it home with me.

His generosity must have been a contagious condition, because many of the men who spent a lot of time with him caught it.

Now, back to us. After our individual first experiences with God, we lived in Las Vegas until the contract ran out (about four or five months), in a roomy condo apartment that had just been built. The apartment owner was a nice man who allowed children, at least he did when we came, but he might have changed his policy after us.

The owner had the surveyors out working the entire day, placing stakes at crucial positions I'm sure, getting ready the second phase of the buildings. Those surveyor stakes had different coloured ribbons tied around them, which probably meant something equally as important as their position. There were at least fifty or sixty of them pounded in the earth in all different places over a couple of acres. After all, they had been at it all day.

Christopher and Timothy had somehow secretly learned to unlock the front door and by the time I got up to give them their breakfast, they had all the 'Hawaiian spears' piled up on the front porch. I wasn't aware of this nor did I fully comprehend its meaning until the sad-eyed landlord rang the doorbell and explained what all those spears were for.

I apologised profusely and I wish I could say that we never caused the nice man any more grief, but two weeks later Christopher and Timothy were with the little beast from across the way who had matches, and they burnt down the large pile of lumber that was to be used to build the new apartments. I'll never forget the look on that poor man's face.

That time in Las Vegas was our last time there. John had decided to quit the show bands and only work at home in Los Angeles or Orange County. We had decided that our family was more important than anything else and the children would be starting school soon; hence no more out-of-town jobs.

Everything had indeed changed for us. We never again talked about or even considered divorce. Whatever the dark thing was that lived on my head like a hat, it was gone, along with the paranoia and fears about nuclear war.

We had quit drinking without realising that we had. And when our friends, Dick and Lynn, drove to Las Vegas to visit us and to bring us a gift of a bottle of expensive Scotch, it worked out well, because during the cold drive over the mountains, they had fortified themselves with just a little sip to keep the frost off. It was about a six-hour drive in those days and it is cold that time of year. They presented us with the empty bottle, shamefaced, heads hanging, but we were delighted to see them.

Dick and Lynn Heying had moved to Yorba Linda a few years before this. Dick Heying was John's oldest and best friend. He was a drummer, a jazz musician, and they had been friends since John was seventeen or eighteen years old. There wasn't much that Dick didn't know about John, or that John didn't know about Dick. They always loved each other. It was Dick and Lynn who went with us when we were married in Riverside.

She was Jewish but didn't know anything about God, and Dick was a gentile who believed in jazz and sports – until Gunner came knocking at their door and patiently opened the Scriptures to them week after week, starting in the Old Testament for Lynn's sake and eventually leading them to Christ.

Dick and Lynn had become Christians a few weeks before, and that is one of the reasons why they had wanted to see us. It was their intention to witness to us. But because of the Scotch, they were too ashamed to bring up the subject, and left the next day feeling completely defeated.

John and I, on the other hand, couldn't get over the change in those two. We wondered to each other, 'What do you suppose happened to them? They were so nice to each other and they didn't say one negative thing about anyone. What do you think? I wonder what's going on.'

Once home again, back in Orange County, we decided to get reservations in the local Catholic school for our boys. We could sense the presence of God in our lives, and so we went back to the only thing we knew. I had been raised a Catholic, though deserting over the 'limbo' issue, and John had almost been an altar boy that one year, so we went back to the Catholic Church.

We were remarried in the Catholic Church because they, of course, didn't recognise the first ceremony, done by the Baptist, in a house, yet! To be married in the church meant I had to go to confession for the first time in fifteen years and that was a hair-raising experience, I can tell you! Probably for the priest as well as me. But in all seriousness, I came out of the confessional knowing that my sins, which were many, were forgiven.

John wasn't becoming a Catholic, so he just had to agree to raise the boys as Catholics and he had to have a few sessions with the priest to settle what that meant. I believe it was supposed to be a six-week course, but the priest cut it short because John would ask all sorts of questions and insist that the priest explain it all before they go any further.

'Well, how do you know it's true? How can you believe something you've never seen? What's your authority? What do you mean, "The Church"? How do you see it personally?' and so on until the man's hands were shaking. John did find out with his many questions, that this poor chain-smoking priest with the shaking hands had just had a nervous breakdown, and had only recently gone back to work.

What a sight we must have been at our second wedding. Catholic weddings are part of the Mass and there we all were, standing up front. Me, in my feather hat, six months pregnant with Stephanie. John, holding the baby, Sean, and us both trying to restrain our two little boys. Christopher and Timothy, whose normal speaking volume went from loud to louder, were straining to break loose from our grip on them, looking around and pointing as if they'd never been in a church before. Which to be fair, was perfectly natural, since they hadn't.

We got through the ceremony without any terrible scene, and I must admit, I felt truly married for real and forever before God.

Right about this time, Dick and Lynn, having worked up the courage to try again, asked us to come to a Bible study at their house in Yorba Linda. We explained that we couldn't because John worked every night but Monday. Dick began stopping by in the daytime once in a while and did his soft sell, while Lynn would call me and urge us to come.

We were going to Mass every Sunday now, and though we didn't understand anything the priest was talking about, it didn't bother us because we didn't know you were supposed to understand church. For us, the virtue of the church experience was in getting all dressed up and in the combined sacrificial effort it took to get the three boys into their church clothes with shoes on the right feet, their bright red hair all slicked down, and to corral them all into the station wagon with no one escaping. And then to sit and stand and kneel at the right places, until it was over.

Our three little red-headed heathens got baptised at that

Catholic church, by the way, which was no easy feat since Christopher was big enough to fight back.

We were just getting used to the Sunday routine, becoming quite confident, in fact, in the stand-ups, sit-downs and kneels, when Sean, the baby, sucking on his full bottle of milk, gave it a hefty yank, pulling the nipple off the bottle altogether and spraying the grim-looking man, sitting behind us, with formula. That was enough of the Catholic Church for us, and we never went back. I'm sure they felt the same way about us, if the look on that man's face as he mopped the milk off with his handkerchief was any indicator.

Timing is everything, and right about then Lynn asked us again to come to the Bible study that was now meeting on Monday night, our night off! What a coincidence! But John was ready for her and explained that he would be very uncomfortable in a group, where everyone knew the Bible but him, but thank you very much anyhow, goodbye. About ten minutes later she called back with the news that everyone in the study had agreed to meet on a different night so that John and I could have the Bible study all by ourselves with Gunner, the teacher. Don't tell me manipulation doesn't work. It worked wonderfully! We were so touched that a group of total strangers would inconvenience themselves just for our sake, and promised we would be there the next Monday night.

3

Salvation and Friends Church
1963–1975

Whenever I remember those beautiful days of our salvation, I can almost smell the orange blossoms again. The whole experience for both of us was indelibly connected to that fragrance that cloaked Yorba Linda in those early days. The dusty warmth of the eucalyptus-lined country roads and everywhere the smell of the citrus trees in bloom. We could smell Yorba Linda three miles before we got there, and the scent would hang on us as we drove back home to Westminster after the Bible study. I already know what heaven smells like; it will be no surprise to me. It smells like Yorba Linda in June of 1963.

Yorba Linda was about five thousand people then, a little town of citrus groves, tucked in the foothills. There was a volunteer fire department, housed in a little building with a pretty park next to it. It had two grocery stores, and we all shopped at the little store because they closed on Sunday, and not at the big, heathen market that stayed open on the Day of Rest. Yorba Linda had one gas station, Barton's Chevrolet, a hardware store, the café where the old-timers hung out, and the three churches: the Quakers, the Methodists and the Baptists. (By the way, for you Brits, the Quakers in the western part of the United States bear no resemblance to what you see in the UK under the same name. OK?)

My ignorance of Protestant churches being fairly complete, when I saw the sign on the Quaker church,

'Friends Church', I thought that it was advertising the quaint way in which everyone seemed to know each other and the friendly way they reached out to people – 'Hi John, Hi Carol, this is Sheldon, the pastor' – that friendly first-name-basis sort of thing.

So there we were in our Sunday best. Me with my feather hat and false eyelashes, because one wore a hat to church, I thought, and it was 1963 and eyelashes were 'in'. And John in his Italian shoes and black suit, looking good, though somewhat like a Las Vegas transplant, as he ground his cigarette into the front step of that little church. He had checked out the entry and hadn't found an ashtray, but had decided to overlook their rudeness, thinking the janitor had forgotten to put it out. I found that I was the only person in there wearing a hat, and I couldn't take it off and stuff it in my purse – the thing was as big as the chicken it was probably made from.

We knew nothing about children's programmes, so we kept our four children, ages six, five, almost two, and six months, with us in the sanctuary. I don't remember what that first sermon was all about and I doubt that anybody else did either; we made so much racket.

Anyone who has heard John's 'testimony' knows his impressions of that first Sunday and I won't go into it again, because many of those dear people that were so good to us are still around, and I don't want to insult them further. Let's just say that for John, it was a 'tight fit'. On the one hand, unendurably uncomfortable with all the religious talk, and on the other, ludicrous, considering the level of musical skill and outdated style of just about everything.

After the 'whole ordeal' was over and he was having his after-church-smoke again on the front lawn, he chided his best friend, Dick Heying, with 'You can't be serious, man! Have you totally lost your sense of humour?' It was at that point of seeing the hurt look in Dick's eyes, that John realised that Dick loved these people and deeply cared about the 'church thing'. So John just shook his head in bewilderment and looked away, pondering what it was that had so changed Dick Heying.

I was having the extreme opposite experience. I loved it all! The out-of-tune choir, the old, out-of-date building, the simply dressed, unpretentious people, so friendly to us, the strangers amongst them – I loved it! For me, it was stepping right into *Friendly Persuasion*, the Jessimine West novel about the Quakers.

It took John some time to adjust to church, but he liked Bible study right away, where he could ask all the questions he wanted and receive a straight answer without all the religious jargon. The time after church, over lunch at Dick and Lynn's house, made it worth the trip for him, because Dick would interpret for John what the preacher had said. 'What the hell was all that about "lamb's blood"? When do they do that? Yuck!' and Dick would explain to him about the sacrificial death of Jesus. 'What's all that Holy Ghost jazz? Sounds weird!' and Dick would do his best to make John understand the Third Person of the Trinity. And so it went, week after week. John's questions getting answered to his satisfaction by Dick, and Lynn making a wonderful lunch for our little well-behaved family of six. I have a scene in my memory of looking for Sean, our two-year-old, and finding him on the top of Lynn's refrigerator. God bless her forever!

In the meantime, I was reading ahead, not waiting for the Bible study. We had this Bible, 'The New English Translation', that we bought a number of years before, thinking every American family should have a Bible, and though we never opened it, we considered it a sort of 'good luck' charm. Well, I had been reading it every morning, during the little ones' naptime, and discovering all sorts of wonderful things. The morning that I discovered that Jesus was the Son of God (think of that in bright neon lights, flashing, with trumpets blaring), I was both stunned and excited to the point that I couldn't wait for John to wake up to tell him my magnificent discovery. I went charging back to our bedroom, shaking John awake.

'John! John! Wake up! Jesus is the Son of God! Jesus is

God's Son!' When I made this announcement to him, he believed me, I think, but didn't really understand the implications.

'So?' was his response (if I remember correctly). 'But John, this changes everything! Don't you see? If this is true, then we need to do something about it!'

'What do we need to do?' he sleepily replied. 'I don't know... I don't know... I don't know! We've got to find out!' I frantically answered. We made plans to ask Gunner all about it the next week at Bible study.

Well, Gunner, the teacher, was just coming to that, anyhow, and he took us all the way from Genesis to Revelation, just showing us Jesus, the Son of God. Wonderful, glorious evenings – coming to life – hearing the words of life – the Son of God breathing into our nostrils the breath of Life.

Keeping Gunner up until 2 o'clock in the morning, chain-smoking and asking questions of that godly layman, a welder by trade, who would get up the next morning at 6 o'clock to start his workday.

You need to know about Gunner to understand John, so let me tell you about him. Gunner Payne, whose real name was Lawrence, had been an oil-rig worker in the 1930s, when he met and married a beautiful Christian girl and came to know Christ for himself. Eventually, his work brought him to the oil fields of Yorba Linda where he started a welding business in a barn behind his extraordinary house. This house that Gunner built for his wife Helen, was constructed of railway sleepers that Gunner had bought and gathered. The huge plate-glass windows with the view of the hills of Yorba Linda came from a derelict gas station that he purchased and disassembled for the use of the window glass. The roof he covered with cedar shingles that he made himself from the tree he cut down for that purpose. The huge, hammered copper fireplace he made was actually a water-heater he designed to heat the water that flowed beneath the brick floor and heated the whole house. All the rooms were made with built-in drawers and cupboards and needed very little furniture. He was also an inventor, and had invented a skip-loader that the beekeepers used to load the hives.

That's how he made money to live. But when we thought of Gunner, it wasn't as an inventor or welder who was a Christian. He was a Christian who was an inventor and welder.

It didn't seem particularly unusual to us that this Christian man made his house entirely with his own hands, invented helpful loading machines, figured out a source of making electricity inexpensively by attaching a sort of float device to the ocean piers that depended only on the waves coming in to work. This man knew Jesus, so of course he could do that sort of thing.

It was our expectation that our bodies and brains would work all together better now that we were with these people who knew Jesus. We expected creative thoughts to flow and would have been disappointed if our garden didn't bloom more profusely than before.

Gunner was just fifty when we met him, a strong and handsome man with thick white hair and piercing black eyes that saw all things, or at least we thought he did. 'Prophet eyes', we call them now. In fact, I started most conversations with him in the middle, assuming he already knew what I was going to say and it would be silly of me to repeat what he must already know, being so close to God and all. I realise now that, most of the time he probably didn't know what on earth I was talking about.

Starting conversations in the middle is off-putting for most people, and I expect that piercing gaze of his could have been merely intense confusion along with determination not to hurt my feelings.

Since John worked at night, we were free in the daytime to drive up to Yorba Linda where God lived, and though we pretended we just liked the area and wanted to have lunch in that nice little park next to the fire station, we always ended up at Gunner's welding shop and interrupted his work.

John would talk to Gunner for hours, asking question after

question, smoking his endless cigarettes, and if Gunner needed to get back to work or if the smoke bothered him, he never let us know. In fact, we had the impression that he had been waiting for us because he loved us so much.

We knew that Jesus talked to him all the time, though he would never say, 'Jesus told me . . .' But he would come over to our house at just the right time to avert a near catastrophe in our still fragile marriage. And we would find him waiting for us in his welding shop when we hadn't even told him we were coming.

Most important of all, he knew when it was our time to be 'born again' and told us so. 'I think it's time', he said one Monday night at Dick and Lynn's house, and we were so relieved because we knew something had to happen. But we didn't know what and nobody would tell us and we couldn't figure it out on our own. There was the spiritual sensation of being full-term pregnant, maybe even late, but not having a clue about childbirth. John and I had puzzled over it. 'How do we join this thing? Is somebody going to tell us? What do you think is supposed to happen? Are we going to wake up one morning and find that it's done?'

Gunner was the very opposite of the hard-sell evangelist. He could have closed the deal months before, but he held back, telling us 'The apple will fall when it's ripe', 'The baby will be born in its time', 'A premature baby is not a healthy baby', etc. It drove us nuts until one night I frantically blurted out, 'Something's got to happen! We believe all this! Can we sign up somewhere or something? Please?' That's when he admitted, 'I think it's time, let's pray.'

Aha! So that was the key! We had to pray! Okay! I was down on my knees first, it's true, and John has said many times, 'Carol was always a step ahead of me', but neither one of us believed that. John just let me 'go first' because I was a woman. Girls first – always the gentleman. I prayed the Catholic Act of Contrition that I remembered from my childhood, 'O my God, I am heartily sorry for having offended Thee, and I detest all of my sins because I fear the loss of heaven and the pains of hell, but most of all because I have offended Thee, my God, who art all good and deserving of all my love', etc., etc. It was the only prayer I could think of that fit, and I prayed it as fast as I could because John was wailing on the floor next to me and it was his turn. He mostly just cried, not knowing any Catholic prayers like I did, but God must have liked the sound of it.

John told me afterward what a fool he had felt, blubbering uncontrollably like he had been, but then he had a flashback to a time when he had been a young musician and needed to borrow some money until pay day and thought of this little drug-dealing drummer he knew who hung around Pershing Square in Los Angeles and always had money. So he went to look for him there and as he was searching the park, along came one of those fanatic types wearing a sign front and back. Kind of an 'eat at Joe's' sort of sign with straps over the shoulders. On the front it said I AM A FOOL FOR CHRIST and on the back, WHOSE FOOL ARE YOU?

It was right there, kneeling on the floor of Dick's house, that John determined how he would spend the rest of his life – a fool for Christ.

As we left Yorba Linda that June night, the fragrance of the citrus blossoms flooding our senses, we saw that there was a full moon with a distinct halo circling it. We knew it was because of us. When we got home we woke up our Christopher, because some six months before he had asked John, 'Daddy, does everybody die?' John, of course, had answered yes, and Christopher came back with 'Even if you're lucky?' So we needed to tell him about Jesus and that 'No, everyone doesn't die, not if you are lucky and belong to Jesus.'

A few weeks before, Gunner had taught on the pearl of great price and the treasure in the field. Afterwards, John told him that he knew of a guy that could only do one thing well and he made his living doing it. Would God require that man to give up his career to become a follower of Jesus? A pregnant silence followed, accompanied by the piercing gaze, and Gunner answered, 'I don't know what God would require of that man, but I believe he would have to be willing to give it all up.'

'That's what I thought,' John quietly murmured.

It wasn't very long until the Lord did speak to John about laying down his career. At first he had thought the issue was just the night-club scene, and John considered taking a job with Disneyland in the department where they placed the different bands in the park, but when we ran it by the old Quaker pastor, Sheldon Newkirk, he said he sensed that there would be something else for John. It seems strange now, looking back on it, that he would just take the opinion of this elderly Christian on something so vital as his means of making a living, but he did – he turned down the Disneyland job – and it would have paid good, too.

Since he believed that God had instructed him to, John quit his job. He explained to his partner, and notified the club owners that he wouldn't be renewing his contract. It was a few months before Christmas that same year, 1963. Not being trained to do anything else, he didn't know where to look. John had this notion that God had told him to quit that job, so, well, God would give him another job. He'd turned down the Disneyland job, and all music jobs were forbidden, apparently, so he would wait for God to tell him what to do. Well, God wasn't telling him anything and everybody around us was getting very anxious. Things were getting mighty desperate for us and we were depleting our resources. I mean to say, we were out of money! Christmas was almost here and Santa was broke!

I remember the scene well. It was one evening during this desperate period and we had been worrying about how we would get through Christmas and pay our bills. I answered the phone when it rang. It was Bill Medley (Righteous Brothers) calling from England where they had gone with the Beatles as a warm-up group, and he wanted John to do a Christmas album with them. All the arranging, total freedom to do it just the way he wanted. Well, I know he did want to! He had always wanted to do a Christmas album, but never had the opportunity. This was the answer to all our prayers! Or was it? John asked me what I thought and I said I thought it was a trap. The devil was trying to buy us back. John thought so too but couldn't tell Bill right then. He hung up, saying he'd let him know. We needed the money so badly and it was the only thing offered since the Disneyland thing – and people, even Christians, were beginning to think we were insane or at least impractical to a criminal degree. It might solve all our problems, unless, of course, it was a trap. Did I tell you they were going to send a five-thousand-dollar deposit right away? Before Christmas? We prayed together and sought the Lord to give us strength to resist the temptation. I knew it was John's decision, but I also knew I could have influenced him negatively. We were frightened. Frightened that we would give in, and frightened over what it would mean if he turned down what might be the last opportunity to work.

After we prayed, John called back Bill's wife and asked her to give Bill the message, 'Thanks, but he couldn't do the Christmas album.'

In the next few weeks, John sold all his horns except one that he traded for a painting he knew I wanted. It was a sad, hard time in our new life as baby Christians.

We had a station wagon in those days and John loaded up the entire vehicle with boxes of music and records and arrangements. His whole lifetime of the work that he loved went into those cartons, and on up to the city dump, where he pushed them out of the back of the station wagon and onto the piles of garbage and other discarded items. It made my heart ache to see him do that. He was totally silent the whole time.

I looked at what he was doing and I thought of the corn of wheat that has to die to bring forth much fruit, and I prayed that some day, one day, God would do something beautiful through John.

We had no knowledge of any other kind of Christianity than the kind Gunner was. 'Lock, stock and barrel, mountain style. No holds barred!' was the way he described God's total ownership of his people, and our need to completely surrender to his Lordship. 'No rights – we gave up our rights at the cross when we gave up our sin. We belong to Jesus now, bought with a price, we are not our own!'

John himself would later describe the same principle by saying, 'I'm change in his pocket. He can spend me any way he wants to.'

Gunner knew nothing of the anaemic Christianity that receives Jesus as saviour but not Lord. It was all or nothing with him, and therefore with us.

We believed this man that taught us about Jesus and what it means to belong to him. We knew from his life that faith in Jesus could keep us through any trouble or tragedy that could happen to us.

About nine years before we met him, his sixteen-year-old daughter had been murdered in an attempted rape. Shot in the back, as she tried to escape. They had named this beautiful daughter Ruby, their jewel.

She was baby-sitting for the children of family friends down the road – citrus farmers like so many of the people here. This family had hired a boy to work in the groves and when warned that this young man had been in jail, they didn't investigate further, wanting to give the boy a chance to start anew. Good people, Christians, Quakers.

It was in the daytime, and the parents were only gone for a few hours. Billy Rupp came in from the groves and found her there. The children saw the whole thing. After the murder, all the men in the community searched the hills for him, and Gunner told us that it was a good thing that he found him first, because the rest of them would have killed that young man.

The *Los Angeles Times* came down to cover the story and the reporter started his article with this statement: 'I think I've just met my first Christian.'

Gunner visited Billy Rupp in jail and led him to Christ before he was executed in the gas chamber. He told us that it was after Ruby's death that he got off the committees and the boards, and instead spent his time going from door to door through Yorba Linda to tell people about Jesus. That's how he came to know Dick and Lynn – just knocked on their door one day. And that's where all these baby Christians in the mid-week study that had given up their night for us had come from – Gunner going from door to door.

Dick used to say that Gunner was the most Christlike man he ever knew, and we had to agree with him. We had been Christians just about six months when Preston, their only son, was in a tragic car accident and though he lived, was severely brain-damaged. This was their brilliant, handsome son. He was the representative for a Christian college and was on his way home when he fell asleep at the wheel.

When we heard about it, our panicked response was fear that Gunner would be destroyed, would fold – become bitter. 'How much can a man take?' We thought. In the midst of all his pain and suffering, he was worried about us and came over to the house to let us see he was all right, that he would make it.

He talked to us until we were calm and reassured us that Jesus was enough to get them through again. 'I don't understand what's happened, but I trust him,' was what he said.

That man was a Christian, and what he was because of Jesus in him, was the strongest argument for Christianity ever stated. He led hundreds of us to the Lord. One to one. He believed that you must win a person to yourself by loving them, before you had the right to tell them what you believe.

'First win them to yourself, then introduce them to your Lord.'

John started going with him as he went from house to house and went with him everywhere he could. He was like Gunner's shadow that first year and a half – Shadow and Echo both – he talked like Gunner, told Gunner's stories, shared the same Scriptures with others that Gunner had shared with him and finally went on Gunner's house-calls himself when Gunner couldn't go anymore because of Preston.

We had sold our house and moved to Yorba Linda in

probably one of the quickest transactions that real estate man had ever conducted. We bought a little house out in what was then country, because we knew it would be perfect for our four children, and it was. I have rare film footage of John working out in the yard of that place. I shouldn't say that because the truth is that John always worked out in every garden we've had. In fact, he designed the landscaping for the mountain cabin we got when he was recovering from the cancer. He actually liked to work outside, found it therapeutic. But our boys swear that they did all the real work and their dad supervised.

It was during this time, in January of 1964, that Penny, my sister, came to stay with us and became a Christian and eventually married Bob Fulton who was youth director at the church. Shari, another sister, wasn't far behind, in January of 1965, and my brother Tim, too. John's mother and stepfather moved up to Yorba Linda to be near us, and they both became Christians. Earl called John one morning after we'd almost given up on them, and stated, 'I'm a Christian! I just realised it! I'm a Christian!' – and he was. Genevieve was very proud and didn't like to admit that there was a time when she hadn't been a Christian, so it was very hard for her to become a Christian. But John believed that when she asked him to baptise her in our pool, that was it, that was the moment of her conversion – although she swore to her dying day that there was never a day she didn't know Jesus. If that was true, she sure knew how to keep a secret! My mother was one of the first converts, and she says she only read the Bible in self-defence and went to this Presbyterian church near where she lived, to prove us wrong. The pastor there answered all her questions and listened to her complaints about John and me being so dogmatic and narrow-minded, and then gently led her to the Lord. God bless that wise man. She too, moved to Yorba Linda to be near the little Quaker church. John took the direct approach with people when it came to witnessing. His approach, at first, was not at all like Gunner's gentle persuasion, but much more confrontational in style. I would cringe as he angered people by explaining to them how dead wrong they were, and how hell was waiting for them. 'I make 'em mad or glad!' he would say with satisfaction.

John soon changed his style of sharing the gospel (more love and less condemnation), and he became very effective in winning people to Christ.

Most of the converts moved to Yorba Linda, just like we did, to be near the church and one another. As you would expect, John did get a job, almost immediately after he took his life's work to the garbage dump, and though it was at a place where they used heavy machinery, a horrible job that he was terrible at (and men got their hands crushed there all the time), it fed and housed us. John has never been mechanical, and he couldn't have been less suited to this job, but God put him there. I don't know what they made at the place and I don't think John did either. It was an experience he had to go through, he said, and it didn't last forever, though it felt like it! He would not quit, either, until God said it was time, no matter how much he wanted to.

'If God's got me nailed to this cross for my good, I'm not going to climb down off the cross and wreck the whole purpose of this painful experience. I'll just go through it, until he's done with me.'

There was a particularly humiliating occurrence when an old friend came to that plant and said he heard that John Wimber was working there, and could someone direct him to his office? They pointed him to the back of the building where John was bent double over an oil drum that he had been cleaning. The old friend came up to John, and not recognising him because of the black oily face, once more asked where John Wimber's office was. When John admitted that the oil drum was his office, the old friend looked at him in horror and disgust. 'What are you doing, man? Have you lost your mind?' John said yes, he had lost his mind and didn't believe he'd ever find it again.

What I find interesting is that he didn't lay down his career for something else. He laid it down because Jesus asked him to. And there was no promise of 'ministry in the future' to soften the decision. It was a sacrifice born of obedience, and that is a key to understanding what motivated John Wimber his whole Christian life.

After John died, I received a letter from an old musician that described something John never spoke about: just what a fine musician and arranger he had been. Let me repeat the letter for you.

Dear Wimber Family,
I'm not a church member, and I haven't seen John since the days at Garlocks Music Store when I was with Mike Patterson and 'The Fugitives', playing bass.

John and I were not close friends, but he has been a significant influence in my wonderful life, and I need to tell you about that.

At the time, around 1962–63, 64? John knew that I aspired to be a part of the music community he was trying to leave behind. He warned me of the 'social dangers' and encouraged me to apply my musical talents in other positive ways. He had hired me on my first record date; I played third trumpet, on the 'My Babe' (Righteous Brothers) album. Louis Leos (So and So's) and George Warner (Disneyland Band) were the other trumpet players, I was thrilled, intimidated, and inspired, all three at the same time, and that's just the beginning.

When Johnny left the Righteous Brothers, I was given his arranging job. My first album project was 'You've Lost That Lovin' Feeling'. I had nothing to do with the title track, but was hired to arrange and play bass on the rest of the album . . .

One of the tunes was Gershwin's 'Summer Time'. I got the credits for a superb arrangement that was performed who knows how many times? A real show-case for the Righteous Brothers . . . Bill Medley in particular. Guess what!? I didn't arrange it, John Wimber did!

I called John and explained, even though I had nothing to do with the mistaken credits. His response was that I should not be concerned, and that I should continue in my new path.

A year or so later, after several tours, and another album, 'Just Once In My Life', I left that job. It wasn't my 'calling' either. I've wished over and over that John's friends and followers could know what he gave up; the years of sacrifice to become a jazz player, to become a fine arranger, and to earn the 'Pop Market' opportunities. He had amazing musical talent, and education, and perseverance.

About a week ago, I figured it out. Thank you John Wimber, and bless your sweet heart.

Sincerely,

Dennis 'Woody' Woodrich

p.s. God, – I hope this is the same John Wimber.

I'm not sure exactly why that letter blessed me the way it has. Maybe it's just someone finally saying it – he was special, really special in his field, and he laid it all down.

God finally let him leave that hand-crushing machine shop and take a job that allowed him to meet new people all the time. His job was to represent a certain bill-collection agency to the physicians through their office staff, but once that was accomplished, he told them about the really important issue of life – knowing Jesus. Soon there was a trail of Bible studies all over Orange County, in all the office buildings where he would go. So many of those men and women became Christians during that rich and fruitful time.

Those were wonderful, foundational years of learning and I wanted them to last forever – leading people to Christ, Gunner there with us, teaching us, caring for us.

There is one scene that stays in my mind because it was so typical of that period in our lives: John and Gunner driving along in Gunner's truck with Jim Campbell, a brand new Christian, in between them talking a mile a minute in his excitement at this whole new life. Gunner turns to John grinning and wryly comments, 'You've got a live one there, John.'

Jim and Laura sold their house and moved to Yorba Linda, too.

It was because of Preston's condition and need for constant care that Gunner and Helen sold their wonderful house and moved away. We understood completely, when he told us that he was leaving, but our hearts were breaking. Especially John's. He didn't know how he could cope with Gunner not being there for him, but also for all the brand new baby Christians that were meeting in our house in Yorba Linda now.

In fact, it was those very concerns that John was talking to the Lord about, that fateful day, walking along the irrigation ditch. How would all these new Christians get along without Gunner? Who would take care of them? Who would teach the Bible study? He was talking out loud to the Lord about all of these issues when he realised that he couldn't understand what he was saying. The words were coming out all wrong. He was speaking in Tongues!

Tongues! What a capital T that stands for Trouble, right here in Yorba Linda!

Well, first off, he should have kept it to himself.

'Carol! I think I was speaking in tongues!'

'Oh no, John! Why do you think so?'

'I was just walking along, talking to the Lord. I didn't mean to – it just happened!'

'Maybe it will go away.' I tried to comfort him.

Gunner was gone so we didn't have to tell him (thank God!). I couldn't help feeling that if Gunner had been here we wouldn't be in this mess now.

This incident was not our first exposure to 'Tongues'. Just about six months before this happened, the young assistant pastor Bill had prayed to be filled with the Holy Spirit, with a similar result. After preaching to these old saints that they knew nothing about being filled with the Holy Spirit and then calling an entire congregational meeting to have it out, once and for all, he fell into the hands of some Witness Lee supporters and the outcome was the eventual departure of the young pastor, taking about thirty people with him to start a church in a home that was connected with the 'The Local Church'. Not a cult exactly but described by Bill himself as the 'terrorists of Christendom'.

Bill had been our friend and the friend of many of the new converts, and if it hadn't been for Gunner and some of the other elders, many more would have left with them. Dick and Lynn and John and I had stood solidly with the elders on that occasion and so there wasn't as much devastation as there might have been. Nevertheless, it was painful and frightening.

Since that had been our only knowledge of the 'tongues' thing, it says something that we didn't immediately throw out the whole experience. John couldn't figure out how he could be praying and talking to the Lord, and yet have the devil jump in. It didn't make sense.

It was during this interim time, while we were still thinking it must be the Lord, and not the devil, that our three-year-old son Sean took off on one of his many escapes (our neighbours called him Gulliver, because of his travels) and got into the beehives at the top of our street. We heard him before we saw him coming over the hill screaming and flailing with hundreds of bees crawling all over him, biting and stinging. We got to him as quickly as we could, John yanking the clothes off of him, because the bees were under his clothes by now, and me brushing the bees off his skin, out of his hair, off his ears, and frantically pulling out stings. He was screaming 'Flies! Flies!'

Our intention was to get him to the hospital as soon as we could get back to the house, realising that he could die from that many stings, and I don't know now why we didn't. John was carrying Sean in his arms and praying in tongues as he took him to our bed and laid him down on it, and he placed his hands on him and continued to pray. I was kneeling down on the opposite side of the bed, listening and watching, thinking John was praying in what sounded like Chinese and watching Sean to see if the swelling would start. Instead of swelling, I watched as the many, many, at least fifty or more, red punctures where we had pulled out stings, started to disappear, until finally there wasn't a mark on him and he was sleeping peacefully. You couldn't even see where he had been stung. We all went to church together that evening, like any other Sunday. But on that particular Sunday, our hearts were full of gratitude to God for saving the life of our little boy.

We were so full of wonder for what God had done that when Sheldon, the elder pastor, came by to see us, we spilled out our joy all over him. How Sean had been healed and John prayed in Chinese and wasn't it wonderful?

Sheldon didn't say a word while we bubbled on. He just watched us and listened until we were through, and then he put his head down and wept. And not from joy, either.

Remember, the church had struggled through the last outbreak of 'tongues', and here it was again. We felt very sorry for him.

It seemed wrong to go against our elders, but we did go to a few Charismatic meetings we were invited to, all the time feeling like teenagers sneaking out without their parents' permission. I'm not sure how John felt about it. Probably differently than I did because he was the one who spoke in tongues, not me, but the tension was getting to me and when I showed John in the Bible that what he had heard at the Charismatic meeting the night before was not scriptural, he had to agree. (There was an interpretation of tongues that was actually a prophecy.)

He told me years later that it wasn't my keen biblical argument that had convinced him. It was what he saw in my face, the evidence of lost sleep and anxiety. It was my trembling hands that made him say we must have made a mistake, and we needed to turn around.

I remember being so relieved, but frightened at how strong and compelling that spirit was. It had felt almost exactly like the Lord. Good thing we had our elders looking out for us.

I somehow had separated Sean's healing from John's

praying in Chinese and, in fact, started to conjecture that perhaps Sean is one of those freaks of nature who are completely immune to bee stings. I was just rolling this theory around in my mind when Sean came running into the house, crying and hopping around. He had stepped on a bee and it was doing what bee stings do to little boys – hurting, turning red and swelling.

I asked God to forgive me for doubting Sean's healing.

So John put his tongues experience away in the file labelled 'Things I don't understand', and left it there and we got on with our life, though I think, for John, a little of the sparkle and joy had been rubbed off.

The word was out though, amongst the Charismatics, that John had been 'baptised in the Holy Spirit' but was staying in 'the closet'.

John's theological understanding then was that he had been baptised in the Holy Spirit when he was born of the Spirit, and that there might be many 'fillings', but only one baptism. I don't think his understanding ever changed on that. He was and continued to be a convinced Evangelical.

But to the Charismatics, every indication of the anointing on John for leading people to Christ or for teaching was attributed to the experience he had with God on the irrigation ditch. He didn't think so, and I simply don't have an opinion now. I did then. I had an opinion on everything.

Every so often I would check with John to see if he could still speak in tongues, or if it had gone away yet. It was always, yes; he could still speak in tongues. It was still in there. I would just shake my head at the mystery of it all. I finally came to the conclusion that it was a psychological response, and therefore not dangerous. I had heard that from Vernon McGee on Christian radio.

All these years I have thought that John and I were on the same page regarding that time in our lives, but now, thinking about it, I don't see how he could have been as convinced as I was that he had been fooled by the enemy, or that it was only a psychological response. After all, he was the one with the experience with God, and I was merely the observer. I think now that he just laid it aside for my sake, and for the sake of the elders that had poured their lives into us, and he waited until a better time.

Years later, when I finally had a similar experience, I was horrified that I had used the influence that I obviously had on John to cause him to put away until later a gift from God.

Eve. I felt like Eve.

But we continued on in our life built around that church that wasn't so little now that so many of our friends had been converted, and we were very happy there. John had started out teaching fourth-grade boys in Sunday School and did so well that they asked him to teach an adult class. He said it was all the same to him – fourth-grade boys or adults. Ten people or four hundred, he said he didn't care – and he really didn't. He proved that over the years. 'I'm change in his pocket. He can spend me any way he wants.'

Ed Piorek, a friend of ours and someone whom John loved in a special way, was speaking recently at our conference, 'New Beginnings'. He was talking about 'Classic Vineyard', holding in his hand the whole time a can of 'Classic Coke' and referring to the 'original formula' that gave Coke its unique taste. He said that he was with John ten years ago when John spoke to a crowd of five thousand and he was with him a year and a half ago when John had been asked to speak at a fundraiser dinner for a radio programme. The hosts had expected 150 and the chairs were all out and the tables set, but only about fifty people showed up. The point was, Ed said, nothing was any different for John whether it was five thousand or fifty. John was happy to be there, he preached the same Kingdom of God (Jesus' right to rule and reign in any given situation), he invited the Spirit of God to come, he had 'words of knowledge' and encouraged the people forward to learn how the Holy Spirit works, and taught them to enter in by healing the sick.

Ed said, 'I want to be like that! The same excitement, the same commitment to the message and call at the end of my ministry as I had at the beginning.' Eddie was with John the day he died and he asked the Lord for that legacy from him.

One day at home a few years ago, John was watching a golf match in his den. I was upstairs watching an old movie called *The Electric Cowboy* about a rodeo champion, a multiple blue-ribbon winner, and the course of his career. Having won these state championships and eventually national championships because he was so good at what he did, he was the headliner wherever he went. As he became older and worn out, his name began to descend on the billboard until, eventually, it was only added on at the bottom of the list as 'also showing', etc. A very melancholy film and it made me feel sad, so I went down to be with John and interrupted his golf television programme and told him about the depressing movie. He looked at me seriously and said, 'That's me, Babe. That is the way life goes. I've told you before but I don't think you really believed me. I do not care how God uses me. I just want to serve him in some way as long as he has me here on earth, and I honestly don't care how.'

When he said that to me, I remembered the night of the fundraiser and how happy he was when he came home. 'Oh, Carol, it was so wonderful! I was tired and had a hard time hearing but the Lord was there. He healed this lady and –' I interrupted him to ask how many had come. 'Oh, not many, probably fifty or so – I felt kind of bad for the hosts – but it was such a great night – the Lord touched almost everybody there. Thank you, Jesus!' This was near the end of his life and he didn't have the drawing power that he'd once had, hence the mere fifty people and the radio programme that didn't succeed. I thought he would have been humiliated or at least disappointed, but he wasn't.

That is the truth, the honest-to-God truth. That is what Ed Piorek saw and wanted for himself.

When he was too ill and weak to preach every Sunday and gave the leadership to a younger, stronger man, it hurt him badly and puzzled him when that man refused John's offer to teach a Sunday School class. John had expected to wind up his life of service in Christ the same way he entered it – teaching a Sunday School class – maybe fourth-grade boys.

John's only ambition was to serve Jesus. He didn't care if he looked the fool; it simply didn't bother him. He didn't think that was important – how he came off. What was important to him was that he serve God. To understand John, you need to know that.

The years in the Friends Church, raising our family, being with old friends and making new friends, teaching the Bible studies, going to church and the picnics afterward at the park, the team effort when one of the group had a 'fish' on the line, a near convert ready to be landed and we all did our thing, just sort of loved and cared for that person until they gave up into the arms of Jesus. Every individual that we met was so precious to us because we believed that it was a divine appointment – that God himself had set up the meeting because he had plans to save that person. It worked out great and once they were Christians, they were part of the team that reeled the new ones in.

Most of us, much of the time, had someone staying with us, as part of that programme. We found that once someone lived with us for a certain amount of time, it was almost automatic that they would be converted – which is saying something very good about our home life even if we weren't consistent with the family devotions! John loved company and he enjoyed a house full of people. He loved children climbing all over him and thoroughly enjoyed talking to people. Sometimes he even let them talk!

Children were drawn to him, maybe because he looked like Santa Claus or a teddy bear. 'Well, how do you do? What's your name again? Good name – good choice! Are you married? No? Why not? What? You're only six years old? I can't believe it! You're putting me on, aren't you? Come on now. Well, what do you do for a living? Are you telling me you don't have a job? How do you get food? Your mommy feeds you? Wow! What a racket!' and so on until the child was almost hysterical. He was wonderful with children and never seemed to tire of the game.

My younger sister Penny, who was eighteen at the time of her conversion, came to stay with us for a number of reasons, but mostly because it was a safe, nurturing environment for growing up baby Christians. She was doing great and just starting to get to know the other young people at church, which we helped along by asking Bob Fulton, the youth director, to watch out for her and make sure she was introduced around to all the nice Christian boys and girls. We could tell he was very conscientious about this because he came over to our house almost every evening to keep us updated on her progress and to talk with us. We were quite impressed with his commitment to our plans for Penny to meet lots of Christians and, hopefully, one day to marry a nice Christian boy; but the late visits were wearing on us, now that John was a day person and I had to get up in the early morning when the kids awoke. We would sit there, the three of us, talking until near midnight when he would finally leave. One night we couldn't take any more and excused ourselves to go to bed when it dawned on us that Bob was coming over to see Penny, not us! We laughed at ourselves for being so dull and prayed that if this was The Plan, then the Lord would bless it. It was and he did.

We had learned from Gunner that our lives were an open book, that we were an epistle written by Jesus to give a lost world hope. It almost sounds like boasting but, in fact, was the exact opposite. He made us see, through his own life, what a life filled with the Sprit of God looks like. The key to living that life was constantly to stay in Jesus and never make the fatal error of thinking we could do it on our own, or that we had become stronger as time progressed and therefore didn't need to be as dependent as we had been at first. No, it was a constant moment-by-moment total dependency on Jesus to live his life through our surrendered lives.

John ran into a former musician friend of his and was challenged and accused by him of needing a 'crutch' to get through life.

'No, man! You've got it all wrong! I don't need a crutch! I

need a whole body conveyance! I am totally dependent on Jesus to get through life!'

From what I've said so far about Gunner, you might have the mistaken idea that he believed in and lived in 'sinless perfection'. If that is what he believed, he was unable to transfer that experience to us.

This is what he believed: a baby may mess himself and stumble as he learns to walk and be a perfect baby for his age. A green apple, not yet ripe, is still a perfect apple for its time. So there was no pressure on us to be something we weren't yet, and we had complete confidence that the Lord was changing us and sanctifying us as we just lived our lives loving him.

Not to get careless, though, Gunner warned, because there is nothing more tragic than an adult that still messes himself and stumbles all over the place – a case of retarded development!

I remember going too far with the Higher Life – I was only about six months old in the Lord and I had been poring over the Book of Romans that morning and saw that sin no longer could reign in my mortal body and therefore I never needed to sin again!

I should have left it at that, but I had the need to do something binding about this revelation, so I wrote out a sort of statement of faith: 'I, Carol Wimber, having understood this day of November, 1963, that according to the Holy Scriptures, there is power to resist sin, and live by the power of the Spirit of God. I therefore proclaim this day that I will never sin again! Signed, Carol Kathleen Wimber.'

When John came home from work and picked it up and read it (I had forgotten to hide it), he laughed at me, not having a religious bone in his body. 'God bless ya', Baby. I hope it works out that way.'

It worked out for about two and a half weeks, until I got fed up and resentful toward a friend we had staying with us, and I lost my sanctification. I tore my Statement of Intention up in little pieces. John noticed, when he came home, that the little paper was gone and figured out what had happened.

He found me and put his arms around me and patted my back. 'Poor love,' he said.

John would often console and help me with little bits of wisdom. 'A disillusioned idealist is prone to cynicism, Carol. Be careful.' He knew me so well and it did help. It always helped.

Years later when I had a dramatic encounter with God, and for a while knew what was going to happen in the future, I became impatient with John because he was making plans for the future that I knew weren't going to be carried out. I was especially frustrated because I knew God had forbidden me to talk about it. John could feel the impatience in my manner and stopped what he was doing, took off his glasses and looked up at me. 'Carol. The trouble that often accompanies those who have been touched by God, is that they begin to look down on those who haven't been touched yet.' I repented.

John was always a realist. A holy and obedient realist. Also, a pragmatist. I'll never forget the look on Sandy Millar's face as John suggested that it would be a good move on the part of the ancient church we were viewing from the cemetery next to it, if they would just lay all those gravestones down flat and use the space for parking!

He was practical in his dress, also. What has come to be a tradition of the Vineyard, the casual dress code, started out merely as John coming to church in whatever he happened to be wearing at the time.

The Quakers have always been known for their plain and simple clothes, but I wonder what George Fox would have thought if he could have looked forward three hundred and fifty years and seen John Wimber going to 'meeting' in his Hawaiian shirt and Bermuda shorts, wearing his soft and comfortable bedroom slippers. I tried to reason with him. 'John, you can't wear that to church!'

'Really? Why not?' I couldn't think of a good answer so he wore what was comfortable to him.

He was also colour-blind and, worse, he was sensitive about it. It actually hurt his feelings if I brought it up, so over the years he came up with some unusual colour combinations. I let the unmatched coloured socks go, saving my interference for a more serious breach of colour law – like the bright lime green summer blazer he bought thinking it was a nice subdued beige.

'You're nuts, Carol. This is beige! The salesman told me so.' And he actually wore that 'beige' coat a number of times until someone teased him about 'as sure as God made little green apples'. It wasn't me, either! I hated to hurt his feelings!

If anyone had ever suggested to John that someday he would be a 'professional pastor' he would have laughed at the idea, or had he even allowed that possibility, he would have been horrified.

For him, it would mean giving up the ministry. It was common knowledge to Gunner and therefore to the rest of us, that the 'professionals' were the least effective Christians around as far as leading people to Christ, and that was the name of the game in our circle.

John Parker, another very effective 'non-professional' minister in the church, would always reply when the board or someone else suggested he become a 'pastor' on the staff: 'I could never cut back to a professional's time schedule. I've got way too much to do with teaching all these Bible studies and raising up all these young Christians, not to mention all the marriage counselling I do. Maybe later, when I'm not so busy ministering to people, I'll think about becoming a "pastor".'

I've watched him over thirty-five years now and I've never seen him without a young couple in tow that he was bringing to Jesus, in his 'office' at the local Polly's Pies restaurant.

These were our elders and that was our mindset, and John Parker expressed it for us very well.

The doors were wide open for John (Wimber) to talk to anyone about Jesus, and everyone he talked to could be honest and disclosing and not feel threatened, but the professionals had a harder time at it. Nobody was relaxed around 'the pastor', and no one could relate with the 'holy man'. Going professional was strategically the worst possible move one could make, if he wanted to stay effective in ministry.

Every young housewife in Yorba Linda knew the terror of seeing the pastor in the black suit, walking up the driveway to call on her. The unnerving part was that it was always without warning. He never gave a hint that one might be on the schedule for that week.

'I'll be by to see you sometime this week', would have been nice because then you would have a chance to at least get the front rooms in some sort of order. As it was, we knew we had exactly twenty seconds flat to put the furniture upright, throw the laundry in the oven, or if that was full, out the back door.

One time he came and I didn't see him until he was at the door because I had been wrestling around on the floor with the kids. I was so frazzled, my hair sticking straight up, that as I leaped to my feet and ran down the hall to put a rubber band around my hair, I stepped on a big carpet needle and couldn't pull it out because it had not only gone through the sole of my shoe, but was firmly lodged in the bone of the ball of my left foot.

All this time the pastor is knocking at the door, and I felt it would be rude to make him wait any longer so I answered the door with the needle skewered into my foot. It was way too late to scream, 'Ouch! Ouch! I stepped on a needle!' That's the sort of thing you say right away, or not at all.

I welcomed him in with my foot raised ever so slightly and asked to be excused and calmly walked back to the kitchen using only my heel on my needle foot and found my pliers (all tools were mine, not John's) and wrenched and pulled that needle until it came loose, without making a sound, I might add, except maybe a mild whimper which I'm sure he didn't hear.

Now, if it had been anybody else but the pastor, I would have acted perfectly normal. I'm sure.

Another thing we all knew was how the religious talk that the 'hired' pastors apparently learned at seminary was a turn-off to most people. It had been hard for John to understand even the Christian-ese term 'saved', except that he had seen the old sign on Angeles Temple in Los Angeles, 'Jesus Saves'. Being a World War II kid, he assumed the sign had been part of the war effort.

Words like 'redemption' were easier for him, having hawked his horns in pawn shops a number of times when he was young and starving and had carried around the redemption tickets in his wallet until he could afford to redeem the instruments.

Needlessly confusing, in his opinion, were 'Ice Cream Social' and 'Fellowship' and 'Sanctuary', and that was precisely the kind of talk at which the pros excelled. Then to make matters worse and to cut themselves off completely from the people they were supposed to bring to Jesus, they wore those black suits!

Musicians also wore black suits, but nobody ever mistook a pastor for a musician.

Thirty or so years later, Bob Jones (a down-home prophetic type) took one look at John and said, 'The Vineyard ain't got no Religion!' and as far as John was concerned, that was true – if we are talking about false piety. He just didn't have it in him.

He did not consider himself a particularly spiritual man, measuring himself by the religious disciplines that were a part of many Christians' lives. In fact, he would jokingly refer to himself as the 'natural man'.

It's rather odd. He prayed regularly, all the time. In fact, he would carry on a conversation with God as if he were talking to Dick, or Bob or me. Without warning, in the midst of a conversation he was having with me, 'Well, Lord, here I am again and I still don't know what you want me to do. I'll wait for you, Lord, to straighten it out. Thanks, Jesus.' He just talked to God, sometimes sitting at the breakfast table with his eyes wide open, looking at the chair on the opposite side of the table, as if the Lord was sitting across from him, listening. Sometimes he knelt down and worshipped, and most of the time he walked around and prayed – always out loud and always with his eyes open. But he didn't think of that as anything 'spiritual'. It was the most natural thing in the world.

John Mumford, national director of the Vineyard in the United Kingdom and Ireland, has said of John: 'What you saw of John in public was exactly what you got in private. There was no "side" to him. There was no sudden change once he came off the platform, whether he was praying for people, or joining in an informal conversation or eating supper. What you saw really was what you got.'

Later in his life, when the gifts of the Holy Spirit were being poured out everywhere he went, he was chided by a prominent Charismatic Baptist for taking a potato-chip break in the middle of a deliverance. 'What are you afraid of?' John asked the Baptist, his mouth spraying potato-chip bits. 'The demon will think I'm rude and leave?'

He read the Scriptures every day and some days he got a lot out of it and other days he didn't.

When he sinned he would confess it to me or to Bob (sometimes to the whole congregation, much to my embarrassment!). He believed that if he immediately confessed even the temptation, he was ensuring he wouldn't give in to it. It seemed to work for him over the years.

His style of praying became my style also. These three-way conversations became deeply important to us over the years as the weight of the decisions we had to make grew with the Vineyard Movement.

The weight of leadership for John didn't seem to have the debilitating effects on him that it has on so many men. He had the attitude that God has drafted him into this job and God would give him the wherewithal to do it.

He told God about everything, and then he told a number of us about everything. He would listen to the counsel of his friends and then he would do what God told him to do. I, personally, took great comfort in that. It was security to me to know that he would always take God's counsel, no matter how much I argued, or how persuasively his friends and counsellors cautioned, or how great the personal cost to him. Over the years, I saw him cut his own throat, again and again, out of obedience. Whatever it is in a person that makes it possible to rationalise the voice of God to make God say what you want to hear – he didn't have that mechanism in him. He always obeyed God. I wish I could shout that from the rooftops. 'He always obeyed God!'

He didn't jump into things without thinking it over for a long time. I would often get impatient with the process and wonder why he was being so slow to act. The difference was, he could see way ahead and was counting the cost. He wasn't a spontaneous or impulsive decision-maker, knowing we would all have to live with the results, but once the decision was made, he would stand by it no matter what the hassle, as long as he believed it was God's direction. When he became convinced that he had been mistaken – which he did on a few occasions – he would take full responsibility and apologise all over the world!

John developed a reputation among the powers that be, of being a good Bible teacher and 'soul-winner'. He was given more and more responsibility until it became quite apparent that something had to give! He was teaching Bible studies four or five nights a week, in homes around the county, and teaching Bible groups at lunch hours in the daytime. Plus, he had to do his job for which he was being paid. That wasn't all of it. We were from the 'you catch 'em, you clean 'em' school. So any time left over was given to raising up and taking care of these new Christians.

John and I both went at this thing like we believed Jesus was coming back a week from Tuesday. Which, of course, we did believe. If not Tuesday, then some time sooner.

Or maybe it was just that it was a harvest time for all of us. So many were coming to the Lord then.

As I sit here thinking about those days, I wonder where all our children were. We didn't leave them with baby-sitters very often, so they must have gone with us. I do remember Gladys Newkirk, the pastor's wife, a very fine and down-to-earth woman, coming by to talk to John one Saturday and playfully (I think it was playfully) poking him on the chest as he backed away from her.

'You don't have any business being gone so much from your family! Why, these little ones need their daddy with them. You just slow down on saving the world, John Wimber! Do you hear me, young man? Do you hear me?'

We did hear her and appreciated her attention and any wisdom she could give to us, young parents without much training. In fact, it was the elders of that church that taught us everything we needed to know about life. I asked Gladys, whose boys were now grown and married, if there was anything she would have done differently in raising her children. I've never forgotten her answer: 'I would stop and smell the roses. I would listen carefully and with interest to my children. I would go for walks with them and not think about anything else while I was with them.'

Me, too. Ditto. That's what you feel like when they are grown up and gone.

It's odd in retrospect, feeling the way we did about the professional ministry, that we even listened when Barney, the new pastor who took Sheldon's place, urged John to come on staff. (That church changed pastors every year.) We had been having such a wonderful time up until then and John was making a good living again working alongside his good friend Dick. I can't remember now what changed our minds, but knowing John and the way he thought it was probably his sense of responsibility that did it.

So, John, on top of all his other activities, went back to school and studied Bible, sociology and archaeology. He didn't give up the ministry to do this, though. Even there at school, he introduced people to Christ, seeing the campus as merely a new fishing pool. He thought it was 'intuition' when he knew the secrets of men's hearts, and a 'hunch that paid off' when he knew the exact words to say that would open a person up to the Lord.

He enjoyed his time at school and so did I because I learned so much church history from him, which has saved us a lot of grief, in my opinion ('there aren't any new truths, just old error').

He was grieved by some of the professors who were unbelieving believers, though. In his later years John said it was at school that the 'magic' faded.

It is hard to know now if it was school or joining the staff of the church with all the added responsibility that shaded the joy with disillusionment, but there was a noticeable, though slight, difference after that time.

If success is measured by how many people were converted after he went back to school and joined the staff, then John was incredibly successful. The classes he taught were always full of new converts that had prayed to receive Christ in one of his home groups. They brought their friends, just like we had. Wherever John taught, the room became too small until they had to open up the social hall that was as big as the sanctuary to house the large group.

It was about this time in our life that an older woman, who had been born into that Quaker church, came tearfully to John and told him he had ruined her church. It was full of strange and unholy young people and it was so crowded she didn't even have her own place any more!

The church launched a building programme right about then and the Ministry and Council (the board) sent a representative over to bring us 'on board', so to speak. They had heard rumours that we didn't like the programme and they wanted to know why. Our take on the whole thing was 'why should we build bigger buildings when the Baptist church is only half full and the Methodists have lots more room for people. Let's fill up every church in town and then think of bigger buildings!' How they could argue with logic and idealism like that, I don't know, but we did see the light eventually and co-operated with the building programme. I know that's true because I'm looking at a newspaper photograph of John and Bob Fulton pointing up to the new rafters on the almost finished new building. The paper is dated 15 August 1970, and it looks like John is wearing his Las Vegas black suit.

Joining the ministerial staff on Sunday will be an assistant pastor, John Wimber of Yorba Linda, member of the church and bible teacher for the past four years. Mr. Wimber will start academic studies toward the ministry as a career this fall. The installation service for Mr. Wimber will be held Sunday at the Main Street sanctuary. Youth minister of the church is Robert Fulton, student at Biola College, La Mirada, who has served for the past two years.

Someone unkindly suggested to John that the reason he had been asked to come on the staff of the church was his enormous influence on so many of the congregation. That may be so, I really don't know, but whatever the truth of the matter, there definitely was the sense, for us at least, of being corralled at last.

They called him Associate to the pastor, then Associate Pastor and, finally, Co-pastor. John, of course, didn't care what they called him. He didn't care about titles or positions and anyhow he knew he was expected to be led and directed by the board, this group of men and women who had not been too crazy about Gunner, who was considered a sort of maverick.

John never had a rebellious thought in his head, or his heart, and he just worked with the different streams of power and authority and did the best job he could for Jesus. That's how he thought of it, and he did a very fine job. That church grew to the largest in our denomination.

He was hurt and dismayed when another pastor confessed to him that he had constantly to fight jealousy because of John's 'golden touch'. He said 'everything John touches turns to gold', and it was hard on him personally. John was stunned by that disclosure because he had never considered that competition was part of the mix.

At times like that we would wonder if we had made a mistake 'going professional'.

That was to be a recurring theme in John's life. The sad and surprising revelation that a friend was in competition with him. Even more hurtful, the friend resenting John because of it.

Maybe it was the lens from which John viewed life that made him different. He didn't think of 'The Ministry' as a career, something he needed to work for and excel at, but as an act of obedience on his part. He was only there because he believed that was what the Lord wanted and it had nothing to do with position or place or power. We still believed that it was a disadvantage to be a professional, but we were willing to put up with it, if that was what God wanted.

Gunner had moved away by now and we couldn't talk these things over with him and, besides, we knew what he thought. He had already declared to us that professional ministry is treacherous water to row through.

As I write this, I'm realising that it may sound more negative than it actually was. These are issues we didn't talk much about at the time they were happening and I'm just now remembering them. Probably I'm overly sensitive to anything that caused John pain, now that he is gone. Like I held my temper for twenty-eight years and now I'm fed up. Well, forgive me. Those few years from 1970, when he joined the staff, to 1974 before he went to Fuller Seminary and met Peter Wagner in a Doctor of Ministry course in church growth, were good years as far as the Kingdom was concerned, even though they may have been dissatisfying for John.

It was during this time that he was asked by Yearly Meeting, to be on the board of church planting, though that isn't what it was called and I can't remember the name of it – but he loved that work.

The Quakers had different terms for everything. Each individual congregation was a 'Monthly Meeting' and the district was a 'Yearly Meeting'. So we were called Yorba Linda Monthly Meeting and we belonged to California Yearly Meeting. Couldn't call it a church because *we* are the church and God does not dwell in buildings made with hands, etc. Quakers didn't go to 'church', they went to 'meeting', and *were* the church. The old Quakers used derisively to call the church-like building 'steeple houses' and, in fact, I just found an old newspaper article about the dedication of the first little church there in Yorba Linda. This was the church of Hannah Nixon, the mother of President Richard Milhouse Nixon. This news piece is charmingly quaint. Let me quote from it here.

> Theodore Stanley and Anna were on their way to the meeting. They were conservative Friends from Ohio and always spoke the plain language at home. He was saying, 'Anna, I don't like the looks of this from the outside or on the inside. On the outside, there is the steeple; it isn't a meetinghouse, it is a church. And on the inside, there is the organ!'
>
> And Anna answered him soothingly, 'Now, Theodore, thee knows it is just a little steeple! And isn't it comforting to hear Edith Steward play "A Shelter in the Time of Storm" on that little organ?' Theodore grunted something in reply, but as they entered the meeting house, they left their prejudices at the door and even joined in the last verse . . .

Of course things had changed since 12 August 1912, and we were pretty much like any other Evangelical church by the time we came to know the Lord, though some of the old terms held on.

We had communion after the manner of Friends, meaning no outward elements, just the quiet contemplation of the body and blood of Jesus and the communion with God and each other that comes from that.

We didn't baptise the new believers in water, believing we were all baptised into Christ when we believed, and the baptism Jesus pointed to was the baptism of the Holy Spirit.

We dressed simply and lived simply and drove Chevrolets, not Cadillacs, though many were wealthy. We had a station wagon because of all our children. Those were the days before seat belts, when you could leap back over the front seat and try to catch the kid that was causing the trouble. I thought of seat belts long before they invented them. They looked like ropes.

We didn't shop on Sundays even though we believed we had entered into our rest in the finished work of Jesus and every day was holy. Wholly his. But Sunday was our day to meet and everyone should be allowed to go to meeting, even the merchants that owned the stores, so we wouldn't add to the problem by shopping on meeting day.

The old Quakers said 'first day, second day . . .' etc., instead of Sunday, Monday, and so on.

We had to go to court once, as new Christians, because they were going to put a beer bar(!) in Yorba Linda and it was against the original Land Grant (as the elders explained to us), and at court the Quakers wouldn't place their right hand on the Bible and 'swear to tell the truth, the whole truth and nothing but the truth'. They said they tell only the truth at all times and they don't need the Bible to reinforce their honesty, as it comes from within, springing from their relationship with Jesus; and to swear to tell the truth is insinuating that there are times they don't speak the truth. Their word is good enough. So the court let them 'affirm' the truth without the Bible as a prop. Yeah! So there!

An old, old Quaker missionary woman, when asked why she didn't drink alcohol when the Bible doesn't prohibit it, answered with a question of her own, semi-quoting Othello: 'Would I put an enemy in my mouth to steal my brains?'

I was impressed by the wisdom of these people and, though John and I were cut from a different cloth – so to speak – we respected and loved our elders, and they loved and cherished us. I think we were kind of like exotic beasts they had brought home and tamed.

The daughter of one of these old families told me after I asked her when she came to know the Lord, 'It was when I saw you and John walk into this building one Sunday looking like the world and I saw what happened to you both when you were converted. It was then, I knew it was true. Jesus is real.'

Salvation and Friends Church 1963–1975

John and I were both teaching Sunday School and since we came early we could watch from an upper balcony as the young couples, our baby Christians, with their little children would stream into church. It blessed us, seeing them, knowing from what God had saved them. We would pray for them, literally over their heads, hidden on the balcony as they carried their babies to Sunday School. For some reason that particular scene – the people streaming into church, the cars changing lanes to get to the driveway leading to the church – always brings tears to my eyes. Most all of those young couples are with us now. A few got away but not very far away, they're in some church somewhere.

We discovered that if we got converts with some sort of church background through the home Bible studies and then very slowly fed them into the church services, they could adapt pretty well. But our friends, mostly musicians, just couldn't do the church thing. They loved Bible study and being with us but they couldn't make the transition into the church. Some could but many couldn't, and it was a source of pain and frustration to John. You can't get there from here, he would say.

Though we loved that little church the way a drowning man would love the boat that he was hauled into, John and I would dream of a church that was designed just for us, the way we like it. No theatrics. Nothing staged. Our kind of music. Songs about Jesus. Casual and simple. Unpretentious and culturally current. Non-religious and transparent and honest. A 'come-as-you-are' gathering, where anyone would fit in, where one wouldn't have to 'dress up' to go to church. Where the leader doesn't look any different than the rest of the people.

Years later after the Vineyard began, a young woman was overheard as she was leaving the gym with her friend. 'It's the greatest church! They don't even have a preacher – the keyboard player just stands up and tells stories!'

No choir, the people will be the choir. Maybe a Big Band, like Count Basie's (that never really happened – yet!).

We'd get rid of all the committees. Put the right people in

the right places. Who are the real pastors? Throw away titles.
Let the ministry be functional. Let's see who the elders are
and not confer that as merit position.

We were just dreaming, not actually planning anything.
We loved our church and would have stayed there forever.
The way it has worked out, that church, those people, have
stayed in us forever. The Vineyard has no idea how very
much they have been influenced by that beautiful, loving
group of Quakers that taught us how to walk.

It wasn't long until the whole counselling load fell on
John's shoulders and even when you're good at it, it's a high-
stress job. He was good at it, exceptional, in fact. He'd cut
right through the prevailing pop-psyche theory and nail the
real issue, and more often than not, the person would be
freed or helped in some significant way. He was so good at
it that people came to the church just because of the
counselling, and sometimes they weren't interested in getting
help at all, but John had a unique way of handling difficult
cases.

I remember, one afternoon, John came out of his office
with a raised eyebrow and a 'help me!' sort of look on his
face.

'Carol, do you have a minute? Come in here.' I followed
him back in to his office where a nice-looking lady was
waiting, looking very uncomfortable.

'Now, Sharon, you need to share with Carol what you just
told me; you know, how your husband doesn't satisfy you
sexually and how that leaves you vulnerable and sexually
stimulated all the time. Carol has great insight with these
sort of sexual issues and I know she would be willing to
help you. Right, Carol?'

Well, you can guess that it wasn't help from me she was
after and she didn't go looking for that sort of 'help' from
the pastor again. At least not this pastor!

I was flipping through John's Bible one afternoon last
week when I was especially missing him and saw 'Carol Kay'
written in large letters in the margin. It was at Proverbs 5:18–
19: 'May your fountain be blessed, and may you rejoice in

the wife of your youth. A loving doe, a graceful deer – may her breasts satisfy you always, may you ever be captivated by her love.' He had underlined it.

That is something you should know about John, if you want to understand him. Fidelity was built into him before he was born. It wasn't even a Christian virtue that had to be developed. It was just always there.

We were content, if not really happy, with the situation until a time when Ministry and Counsel hired a consultant to the staff, in an effort to make Barney do something they thought he should do. 'Light a fire under Barney' is a phrase that I heard. It's hard to remember now exactly what it was and it isn't important. What is important to this story is that the consultant Kendal Dance (surprise! not his real name) was a rabid, positive faith, name-it-and-claim-it, take-authority-over-your-life, God-loves-the-strong-and-ignores-the-weak-underachievers kind of believer. If you were sick, then claim God's promises and declare yourself well! God is bound by his word and he has to co-operate if you meet the requirements: declaring his word to him. God loves a winner!

He wanted testimony time in the morning service to include those who had been successful and achieved high status in life. It was the old prosperity doctrine, but this little group of unsuspecting Quakers didn't recognise it because they had never heard of it. Kendal was full of wise-sounding slogans: the journey is the goal, the seed draws to itself what it needs to grow, and on and on. We had never been so unhappy since we had become Christians. The church felt like a business and we were disheartened by what was happening to it.

John enrolled in Peter Wager's Doctor of Ministry course in church growth at Fuller Theological Seminary and was fascinated by the study of churches. It was the first time he had been exposed to any church other than our own, and it opened him up to the whole glorious church. He loved it. When Peter Wagner, who knew of John's work in his own denomination, offered him a job to establish the Charles E. Fuller Institute of Evangelism and Church Growth, he decided to take it and resigned from the Friends Church. Though we knew it would be a tough adjustment for our friends, we comforted ourselves, along with them, by reminding them that we weren't going to go anywhere. We would still be there every Sunday and nothing much would change. Everything changed. It was as if the heart of the church was gone.

John said in *Power Evangelism* that this happened in 1974, but Peter Wagner said it happened in 1975. I'm going with Peter because John was no better at dates than I am.

In reading through this again, I realised that I had completely left out the ongoing problem of the Charismatic experience and how to discourage it. It was a perplexing problem for John as well as for me. It must have been much more confusing to John, having experienced the Holy Spirit that one day as he walked along the irrigation ditch, than it was for me, who had experienced nothing but had a strong opinion nonetheless.

During these years, 1963 to 1974 (depending on who you're going to believe: Peter or John), Calvary Chapel (a large church springing up from the Jesus People Movement) was at its zenith with the hippies coming to Christ. Melodyland, a huge Charismatic revival centre, was only a few miles away. We did our best to keep the new Christians away from those hotbeds of error, but it was increasingly hard. Some of them would just slip right out of our hands after conversion, like a greased pig, and into the Charismatic thing before we even had a chance to protect them by our wise and prudent counsel. We were losing too many to the enemy, so Ministry and Counsel decided to make a focused study on the problem and appointed me as a sort of expert witness because I had grappled with the issue for so many years. I reported to them that the spirit that controls this thing was the most powerful spirit that I had ever encountered. Almost irresistible, in fact, and if the new Christian was not forewarned, he would surely be seduced by it. Even being forewarned, the chances of survival were increasingly slim. I felt as if our church was one of the last bastions of sanity in this wave of charisma that was flooding the churches. Oh, worry, worry. It was a good thing I was there to guard the light.

Interestingly, at the time, I thought John had the same fix on the problem that I did – that he and I saw things the same way. In retrospect, I realise that John was really quite silent the whole time. (I thought he thought like I thought. Now I think he 'thunk' his own thoughts.)

4

Fuller and the Beginning
1975–1977

Can you even imagine the new vistas that opened up for John and then for me, through John, as he was exposed to the whole church after knowing only our own little denomination? It was something like what Galileo must have felt when he gazed through his refracting telescope and discovered that we were not the centre of the universe, as we had thought – we were merely a mid-size little planet, circling the centre. After the initial shock of discovery, it was really quite wonderful. The rich tapestry of the church of Jesus Christ. All the different denominations, the diverse groups, expressing their worship in manifold ways.

The years John spent with Fuller experiencing and studying churches was probably the most valuable education he could have designed, if we had known what God was getting ready to do.

Peter Wagner is a wonderful, enthusiastic believer, and he never met a church he didn't like. John told me that it got to be a joke with the church growth team. They would be at a new church – say a Presbyterian church – and halfway through their service, Peter would whisper to John, 'John, you know, if I lived here I would go to this church! Isn't this a wonderful group?' Then the next time with the River Brethren, 'John, if I lived here, this is where I would attend church.' The next week at Church of God, 'John,' he whispered, 'don't you love this place? This is where I would go if I lived in the area.' A few years later Peter came down to visit us at the Vineyard and he raved about the church; he loved it and if he lived closer he would go to the Vineyard.

He wasn't fickle; he simply loved every expression of the church of Jesus Christ. Apparently it was extremely contagious, because John also came down with a severe case of 'whole-church love' and never got over it. There was only one exception, and that was a snake-handling group from the hills in the Appalachia Mountains.

John and Peter had brought a group of students with them on a field trip to study this little-known church. Their church meetings were not advertised, of course, as this brand of fundamentalism was outlawed years ago. They had sent a guide to bring the Fuller Seminary group up the winding paths in the woods to where they met. I asked John to describe the whole experience in detail and the first comment he made was that he thought the music was strange – worked up – fleshly. Not anointed, he concluded. I thought it strange that out of all that was going on around him, he noticed the music. The leader greeted the 'visitors from Pasadena' and asked if they would come up to the pulpit and give a greeting, as was their custom with visitors from other churches. Well, this was no ordinary polite invitation; it was more along the lines of a challenge to the 'book-learned-folk-from-the-seminary' cemetery, Har! Har! out west'. The pulpit was not your ordinary pulpit either. It was more of a shallow-sided box, up on a stand, with a dozen or more extremely poisonous snakes squirming around frantically in the hopes that one of these suckers from the seminary would place their hand in harm's way! Peter passed. Eddy Gibbs, who was with the team, commented, 'Naa, I'll start with worms', so that left John to save face for the visitors. He told me he prayed about it and the Lord gave him the go-ahead sign, so he went forward and stood mere inches from that mass of squirming snakes, which they had made clear were fresh-caught-today snakes and not your old worn-out half-tamed snakes, like some groups had who were not true believers. Without flinching or leaping backwards as the snakes raised their heads, having smelled Southern

California blood, John delivered a greeting from the group and expressed their thanks for being invited to this meeting. He ignored the snakes completely and was welcomed back to his seat with some hearty back-clapping and hand-shaking and not a little relief, I'm sure. The leader, possibly frustrated by now, mixed up a big mason jar of rat poison and creek water and drank it down in one pass with a triumphant smile after a reading from their foundational text, the Gospel of Mark, chapter 16, verses 17 and 18: 'And these signs shall follow them that believe; In my name shall they cast out devils; they shall speak with new tongues; they shall take up serpents; and if they drink any deadly thing, it shall not hurt them; they shall lay hands on the sick, and they shall recover' (Authorised Version).

John said that the man who drank the poison slowed down considerably like a tape-recorder that needs new batteries, but he didn't stop talking. They all watched as his face changed colour from grey to red to deep purple, but he held on. He stood up there holding his tattered Bible upside down, quoting from memory the verses that were important to them. John said most of them couldn't read but their Bibles were precious to them, nonetheless. I asked him if there was anything redeeming in the experience and he said that he spoke with this old woman after the service and she recounted how as a small child, lying on her mother's lap, when the snake box was passed around, she would watch her mother's face as she placed her hand down into that box. Radiant with adoration, this was the way she showed her faith in Jesus. It was notable that she never got bitten. John said he understood better the roots of these people after talking with the old woman, but he did notice that the present leader was missing fingers on both hands!

It was a fascinating study, but Peter never said, 'John, if I lived in these hills, and couldn't read or write and if I were extremely ignorant, I would go to this church!'

Something on the opposite end of the scale were the Lutherans that smoked cigars and drank beer, but loved Jesus! We had been converted to tee-totalism, no alcohol at all, when we were converted to Jesus, so the whole idea was a completely new one to us, though we knew that the prohibition in Scripture is against drunkenness, not alcohol in general. He told me about a lunch that day with these Lutherans, and how one of them had led the cocktail waitress to the Lord! Smoking his cigar and drinking his beer in the same breath! I was amazed as one more legalistic brick fell off the wall that separated us from the rest of Christianity.

John was often gone half the week but he would call me daily and report what he had seen and learned that day about the diversity of the church. One phone call in particular will always stay fresh in my memory because of the foundational effect it had in the Vineyard and our philosophy concerning the ministry to the poor.

John had been a part of a huge multi-regional meeting of the Church of God, somewhere in the south. The old evangelist had long since blown out his vocal cords as he called the people back to their commitment to the poor. He was pleading with the people to remember their roots, that they were called to feed the hungry and that's where they began. They were called to clothe the naked and bathe the babies and go visit the sick and bring them food. But they had left their call, their first love, and now they were driving fancy cars and dressing up like the world, building fine monuments to themselves while all the time the poor, whom they had been called to, were left destitute. It wasn't the eloquence of the evangelist – John said that his message was extremely simple and his voice so hoarse, he was hard to hear – it was the power of the Holy Spirit.

John described how the people would bend with that power and moan with the weight of conviction of sin, and as the evangelist continued on, unrelenting, they would sway in the opposite direction, all together as one person – like wind over a field of wheat.

John said it was the most powerful thing he had ever been a part of, and as he was telling me about it, he was weeping. 'Carol, if God ever has me pastor a church again, I pray we will devote ourselves to the poor.' As he wept and described the meeting to me, I felt as though I had been there with him. He had been up all night reading Isaiah 58, the true fast, and he was under a heavy conviction in respect to the poor. As he was telling me about it, he just started praying right then on the phone, commiting himself to God's heart for the poor and weeping the whole time.

That is why the poor have had such a primary place in our understanding of ministry. It started with whatever God did to John in that tent with those people who had begun as poor simple farmers that served Jesus by helping the even poorer among them, but had now lost their way and left their call as God prospered them.

I loved that about John; he never got sophisticated. He was never self-conscious. He was never ashamed to let his simple love for Jesus show, to me or to anyone else. It didn't matter; he was the same with everyone, whoever he was with.

His life during the church-growth years had its drawbacks (one can't be gone a third of the year and still be totally tuned into things at home), but he learned vitally important principles about the church and how it grows. Just as important, why it doesn't. 'Only Jesus can grow his church. If it isn't growing, then let's identify the problem and remove the obstacle', or something like that. 'There is no such thing as a "dead" church. If it is the church, it is alive and will reproduce unless something is stopping the process', or something like that. I used to know all that church-growth stuff, but it's been too many years now.

It was an education and we were grateful for it, but there were some disillusioning aspects to it. I noticed one morning that John seemed overly weary and I asked him what he was thinking.

'I've almost come to the conclusion that God honours ambition and ego, because that's about all I find out there.' That was a sad thought and we spent the day being sad over it.

Every once in a while, he would come across a church

that was growing for no apparent human reason. Effortlessly. These churches were the ones that captured John's interest. A sovereign work of God, a move of the Spirit. It wasn't the teaching or the programme or the building, or anything man had a hand in doing. It was just plain God and it was wonderful. John told me of one church that met in a big rodeo hall. John and the team arrived there fairly early but the parking lot was already filling up and the people were running up to the entry, unable to contain their excitement. What was the secret ingredient?

That story came back to my memory early one Sunday morning a few years later when the Vineyard had started, as I was parking the car in front of the Canyon High School gymnasium, where we met in those days. It was still early but the parking lot was almost full and I found myself running up to the doors along with the others, unable to hide my joy. God was going to meet us there and we could hardly wait! We had found the secret! No, the secret had found us.

This went on for a few years, John flying here and there. He discovered the meaning of flying a 'red eye'. (It has to do with the effect on your eyes of those all-night flights.) Most weekends he was home so we would still go to our church, but it wasn't easy because the attendance declined after John left and we worried about the church. We had a cabin in the mountains that we bought with the idea of retiring there one day. We would spend some weekends up there when we could work it out with our children's schedules. Our children, by the way, were growing up by this time. Christopher and Timothy were in high school. Sean and Stephanie in junior high school. We quit referring to them as 'the boys' (Chris and Tim) and 'the babies' (Sean and Stephanie), as we always had. 'You get the babies, Carol, I'll find the boys.' They were in sets, with three years separating the sets, so close in age that they looked like twins. Sean, who was so close to John, was more severely affected by John's absence than we realised. It became apparent after a while that our lifestyle wasn't working out for our children, so John considered taking a position with a parachurch organisation that was based near our mountain house.

In telling his story, he has said how spiritually dull he felt during that time. I do know that he was somewhat disillusioned and that he would ask me to pray for his concerns for the particular church that needed help, rather than praying himself. I know how worn out with the travelling he was, and how tired. He was also very successful and that somehow made it worse for him. He told me that on one occasion after the seminar was over, they gave him a standing ovation and the applause was still going on as he gathered up his notebooks and left. He met his colleague waiting for him in the hall and he was weeping. John asked him why he was so emotional and he answered, 'No one but Jesus should be applauded like that.' They could still hear the applause as they left for the airport and John was heartsick. Not only heartsick – his body was not doing so well either. It was about this time that God gave him a promise from Psalm 61:

Hear my cry, O God; listen to my prayer. From the ends of the earth I call to you, I call as my heart grows faint; lead me to the rock that is higher than I. For you have been my refuge, a strong tower against the foe. I long to dwell in your tent for ever and take refuge in the shelter of your wings. For you have heard my vows, O God; you have given me the heritage of those who fear your name. Increase the days of the king's life, his years for many generations. May he be enthroned in God's presence for ever; appoint your love and faithfulness to protect him. Then will I ever sing praise to your name and fulfil my vows day after day.

He has it underlined in his Bible. Every verse, in wavy lines, because he was on a bumpy plane somewhere at the ends of the earth when God spoke to him.

Which reminds me of a time when he was flying somewhere – I can't remember now and I couldn't remember then.

My mother called me that night and said, 'Isn't John on his way to Atlanta? A jet just went down in a hurricane there!' I calmed her down with, 'Oh, no, Mom. He's in Denver. When he calls I'll tell him to stay out of Atlanta. Ha, ha. Now don't you worry about those things.' Silly little mom. Well, he was on his way to Atlanta, and the plane that crashed was the one that landed three minutes before his! He told me about being on that plane and trying to finish his notes before they landed. Everyone was going nuts as the plane was tossed around in the hurricane and the man next to him was downing one whisky after another and staring with unbelief at John who was scribbling his notes. 'My God, man! Don't you realise what's going on here?' he screamed at John. John calmly turned and looked at him and answered, 'You don't understand. If this plane crashes, I don't have any problem at all. I'm going to heaven. But if we land and I don't have my notes done, I've got a real problem.' He continued writing while they made a messy but successful landing.

There was another time he barely escaped death. He was scheduled for a church-growth thing in Colorado and was driving up the highway to Estes Park in the Rockies, and he noticed that his was the only car going up the hill. All the rest, and there were a mass of them, were going down the hill. Racing down, in fact, and some were honking their horns at John and making frantic hand motions of a 'go back' sort. He drove blithely on for a while but did turn on the radio in time to hear about the dam that broke. He made the fastest U-turn in history – his history, at least. Lots of people died that day and I was grateful that John was not one of them.

During this intermittent time with Fuller, after leaving the Friends Church staff and before the actual beginning of the Vineyard, there were a number of occurrences that culminated with our being invited to leave our denomination. Keep in mind that our church had a cessationist view about the gifts of the Spirit, and we had done our part to make it that way.

One important ingredient was the breakdown of our prejudices against Pentecostals and Charismatics. Just studying the revivals around the world and talking with dozens of missionaries who had been there and had seen what God was doing was enough to open up our closed minds to a part of the church that we had simply ignored. Chuck Kraft, also at Fuller, had been a missionary in Nigeria. He told John how he had prepared a study on the Epistle to the Romans for the leaders there, only to have them come up to him afterwards, in frustration, to complain that they needed to know how the gospel could help them deal with the demons that hassled them. John talked to one missionary after another who told him of a completely different world-view that conflicted with our western, rational mindset, and how the missionaries couldn't share the things they had encountered on the field when they came back home because the western church found it too difficult to believe. Paul Hiebert, a professor of anthropology at Fuller, had been a missionary in India. John heard from him that most non-westerners have no word for 'supernatural' because it is perceived to be natural for spirits to interact and affect our lives. Through these men, John was exposed to a different way to perceive life and to doubt his own assumptions about spiritual reality.

Listening to these missionary professors, as well as students from Third World countries, certainly had its affect on John's world-view. He heard, for the first time ever, dramatic stories of healings and miracles, all that while being exposed to George Eldon Ladd's teaching on the Kingdom of God. The already, and the not-yet. The invasion of the Kingdom of God into this present evil age. Now, we *taste* of the powers of the coming age, caught between two ages, this present evil age and the age to come, we experience the *intermittent* reign and rule of the King, right now, here in any given situation. Of course, John took it further than Ladd had intended, right into the arena of everyday life. He expected the King to rule when he preached the gospel of the Kingdom.

Another thing that influenced John was working with Peter Wagner, who was definitely a believer in the gifts of the Spirit. He had been a missionary in the Friends denomination, our very own California Yearly meeting, though he was at that time a member of Lake Avenue Congregational Church.

There was John Amstutz, who came to work with John at Fuller. He had been a missionary and was a member of the FourSquare church where Jack Hayford pastored. He was a Pentecostal and a godly, deeply spiritual man. It was John who had wept when John got the standing ovation. I asked my John if he would recommend a book on the Holy Spirit for me, because I really needed to understand some things. John told me he trusted John Amstutz and would ask him for a book list. John didn't give me a book list; he gave me his very own books to read, ones that he had taken on the mission field. These were just the classic theology textbooks, like Owen's *The Holy Spirit*. What undid me were the personal notes that John Amstutz had written in the margins – prayers and petitions for the Spirit of God to move. One note echoed the cry of my heart, 'Oh, God, have mercy on us!'

There was that time that God spoke to John so clearly, and I don't know whose line it was originally; but it so struck John that it became his own word from the Lord. 'I've seen your ministry (with an 'I'm not very impressed' attitude), and now I'm going to show you mine.'

There were those special kinds of churches that defied explanation as to the reason for their success. The effortless ones, John couldn't explain and he couldn't understand but, most of all, he couldn't forget.

It was at this time that I had an alarming dream in which I was standing on a wooden box and I was preaching on the subjects of the gifts of the Spirit. In my dream, I had ended the confusion for all listening to me by explaining to one and all that the gifts of the Spirit were divided up equally by tenths. There were ten gifts – I named them – and one-tenth of the people had the gift of healing, one-tenth had the gift of teaching/prophecy, one-tenth had the gift of helps, etc. When I got down to tongues – which I was liberally allowing one-tenth to have as long as it was used as a missionary gift – something like a hot electric wind hit me and went through my mouth and nose and eyes and seared through my whole body and then came back out my mouth in uncontrolled (by me) tongues speaking! My own voice, speaking in tongues, woke me up and I was shocked and amazed and somewhat bewildered by it. It was just a dream but I was still speaking, though wide awake. I woke up John and asked him, 'Good grief, John! Did you hear that? I think I was speaking in tongues!' He asked me if I could still do it and I said, 'Certainly not!' and he went back to sleep. I gave no credence to dreams, of course, and intellectually I was still in the same place. Yet, something had happened to my confidence in my own understanding of God and how he works. My know-it-all attitude was like a sandbag with a hole in it and I was losing sand fast.

I started thinking about and remembering John and the experience at the irrigation ditch when we were new Christians. I thought a whole lot about how I had influenced him to deny that encounter with what just might have been God after all! What if I had been wrong?

Another factor was our yearly denominational camp at Quaker Meadow where John was speaking, and that reliable Quaker pastor, a friend of John's in whom he had confidence, asked him to listen to this lady from his church who said she had a 'word from God for John'.

We didn't even use that kind of language. 'Oh, come on, Ray. I've had enough of unhappy middle-aged women in my years of handling the counselling.'

Ray said, 'No, John. I know this woman and if she says she has a word from God for you, she has a word from God for you. Trust me.' So John agreed to meet her half an hour before the next session at the top of the little hill by the amphitheatre. They met and she didn't say anything but sat down on the bench. John was trying to be a good sport so he sat down on the bench also and waited. And waited and waited. Then he waited some more. She wasn't saying a word but the tears were beginning to flow down her cheeks. John went from discomfort to extreme embarrassment and, finally, past that to impatient irritation. She went from tears to outright weeping to out loud wailing. 'Lady!' he said in exasperation, 'I've got to teach this next session. You've been crying for half an hour! Your pastor said you had a word from God to me! If you have a word, what is it?' And she stopped crying, turned and looked at him full in the face for a few moments. 'That was it,' she replied. She got up and started down the hill. John was stunned. The idea that God cried over him hit him in the heart like a sledgehammer. He has said that he could have understood God being disappointed in him, or even God being angry with him, but weeping over him? It undid him and he was very distracted and near tears during his next teaching session.

John told me about it later that afternoon and I was quite excited over the idea that God might talk to John, even though the message seemed odd. I didn't realise until later how shaken John was. The next day the woman came up to us and said she had something else to say to him. 'John has not been using the authority that God had given to him. God wants to know "Are you going to use the authority or not?" ' We puzzled over what it could mean. 'What authority? Quakers don't have any authority,' we said to each other. The day we were leaving the camp, she came up to us again and said, 'There would be those who you (John) would consider friends and they would attempt to censor you (John). You (John) are not to take a human point of view in defending yourself, but God would raise up those to defend you.' Then she quoted the text from Matthew, 'Don't worry about what you will say when you're brought before kings and magistrates. It will be given you what to say.'

I remember thinking, 'What could she be talking about? John doesn't have an enemy in the world! Everybody loves him.'

All these things happened sometime in 1976 and culminated in September at the camp, and then reached the point of no return when I had a most painful, powerful encounter with the Living God. It left me totally unravelled but bursting and overflowing with the Holy Spirit. My strange dream had left me unsure about my view of spiritual things, so one day I decided to ask God about it. 'What went wrong, Lord? Is this the way you wanted it to be for the church, for John, for me?' I was talking to him as I was walking back into the house from the back garden. By the time I got to our bedroom where I pray, I could hardly breathe because of the weight of conviction of sin. I realised without a doubt that John had encountered the Lord that day thirteen years before and I had influenced him to deny the experience. I saw John with a gaping wound, unhealed, and I was so sorry. I thought of all the young Christians whom I had discouraged from spiritual experiences – being the self-appointed 'keeper of the light' – all those years. What had my attitude cost our friends? I was so deeply aware of my pride and arrogance and my sheer stupidity in thinking that I could determine what was 'of God' and what wasn't. Sadly, the criterion had always been, 'Can I relate to this?' As if my experience in the Lord was some sort of plumbline. I was so ashamed and I felt the weight of guilt to the point that I couldn't quit crying. All day, all night, the tears would run. I wore dark glasses and didn't go anywhere except to the grocery store. (I still had my family that needed to be fed.) Fortunately, John was gone almost three weeks, so he didn't notice. I knew he would think I has having a nervous breakdown and, frankly, I thought I was having a nervous breakdown. I had never been like this, ever, in my whole life. It was during this time of my meltdown that John called from the Church of God conference and cried about the poor. I was in such a state that I resigned from the board with the explanation that I didn't trust any of my thoughts any more, and I stalled when the women wanted to start up the women's Bible study again.

I realised one night as I was praying and repenting that I could speak in tongues. My first thought was, 'Oh, is this what all the flap is about? Any Christian can do that! It's very natural, not strange at all.' I tested it. I could start or stop. Didn't have a clue what I was saying but thought it was interesting that this phenomenon was what churches were splitting over, something so unthreatening and un-weird. I put it aside and went on praying for the church and repenting for my hardness of heart, and what it had cost John and the rest of our church. There were times I thought my heart would literally break with the weight of sin and the realisation of my deadly influence on John and those around me. I remember thinking that if this is the baptism of the Holy Spirit, I don't know how anyone lives through it. I knew it was God, or I knew I had gone crazy. Maybe both.

This went on with me for maybe two weeks and then God lifted it all. I knew I was forgiven and he was going to fix it. He was going to do what he had intended in the beginning with all of us. My tears dried up and I cannot describe the overwhelming gratitude and hope I had for our future. There were a thousand things I understood in a moment of time and the Lord showed me the future, our future – What he was going to do with us and the part that John had in it all. God was going to put the puzzle together himself and he would put John in the place he had to be. I figured we were going to be asked to leave the Friends Church, because I 'saw' us all getting baptised in our pool. (Friends don't water-baptise.) I saw many, many things during that time in my life, but this is John's story and I want to stick to the subject.

When John came home from that long trip, he might have thought he had walked into the wrong house: I was so extra loving and kind to him. I couldn't look at him without seeing the gaping wound in his spirit – for which I was responsible. I wanted to run to him and ask him to forgive me for talking him out of his encounter with God, and I wanted to tell him that it was the Holy Spirit all those years ago that enabled him to speak in tongues, and not a psychological quirk as I had tried to make him believe; but I couldn't. I couldn't say any of that. I knew that I had abused my influence on him that time years ago and I wasn't allowed to use my influence for good now that I realised how wrong I had been. I knew that if it were God, he would influence John, himself, without any help from me. So I just shut up and loved him, prayed for all of us and waited for the promise of God.

Late September or early October, I started teaching the women's group again, with the team of my closest friends. Bob Fulton started up the fellowship meeting of the leaders and teachers that John had introduced the previous year, for praying and encouraging one another. We had all been so busy with the work of the church that we were worn out and needed refreshing. We had met a few times and it was good, but John's travels made it impossible to continue. So, now, a year later, Bob Fulton and some of the other leaders and teachers arranged for a night a week to get together. It was wonderful right from the first meeting, but I only know that second-hand because, although I was invited, I knew what I had gone through with the Lord was still too evident and I would frighten them. (I would liken it to Moses who had to wear the veil because his face shone so bright, but my encounter with the Living God had to do with conviction of sin, not the Ten Commandments.) I knew this was the beginning of what God had promised and I was ecstatic, even not being there.

I wish I could describe for you that women's Bible study. I knew that the fear of the gifts of the Spirit had quenched the flow of the Holy Spirit before and I also knew these women trusted me. I felt the key was to present Jesus and his love in the clearest way I could and, in that love, fear wouldn't have a chance and the gifts wouldn't be a problem any more. The Lord could have his way and we would all be filled with the Holy Spirit without even realising it until it was too late. That's exactly what happened! Everyone was so fully in love with Jesus that by the time the Holy Spirit was presented, they were filled with his Holy Spirit without even remembering that they didn't believe in it. As each one of the teachers had this encounter with the Lord, they would teach the next week. They didn't teach about their experience, they were teaching the Gospel of John and stuck to the text. But the text always had just the right message for that day and it was the most powerful time. I, of course, was aware that we would eventually be busted by Ministry and Counsel, so we 'made hay while the sun shined', as they say in Missouri.

By then I was sane enough to go to the meeting that someone called 'Afterglow', and God was there and we basked in the joy of it all. It was there that Bob and the rest of us laid down the rules for this group of us 'rule-makers'. One: No prayer requests for anyone else but yourself; you are here for you, not for anyone else. Two: We are going to sing to God, not about him, and we are going to learn to worship, whatever that means. Three: Different ones will share and no one will monopolise. Four: No bringing up church problems and no church criticism. Five: Let's leave our places and positions and trophies and badges and honours at the door, and all come together on equal ground while God teaches us about himself.

Well, you can't have that kind of meeting without the Lord showing up. Before long, it became a problem to the church. I think most of us believed this was the revival that we Quakers had been praying for, and we changed the meeting to Sunday night after evening church – thinking that people would come back to church, if only for the purpose of going to the meeting afterwards at a house just down the block. Well, it did have the effect of filling up Sunday night church, but the elders smelled a rat and sent Barney over to check us out. He came and took his appraisal back to Ministry and Counsel: 'It's the Lord.' Ministry and Counsel sent Barney back with an edict to shut the meeting down. Barney came again and said he hadn't worshipped like that for years and he went back to Ministry and Counsel and announced, 'I can't do it. It's the Lord.' They fired him and he moved away.

John, whatever he has said, only missed the first five meetings. When he came the first time, I asked him afterward what he thought of it. He said it was nice but it wouldn't go anywhere because it didn't have any leadership.

The week before that, I had gone to the meeting after apologising to John for my terrible temper. I didn't notice that I left him with his mouth hanging open in wonder! What preceded this was me coming home and finding Christopher washing his carburettor in the kitchen sink. I yelled at him to 'get that filthy thing out of the house and never to wash engine parts in my kitchen sink again. Do you hear me, young man? Never! Never! Never!' or something along that line. John came in from the family room to see what the ruckus was all about and listened for a while. Christopher left with his carburettor and I was muttering as I cleaned the engine grease out of the sink, 'How many times have I told that kid not to . . .' when John quietly interrupted me with the infamous words, 'Carol, you've ruled this house with your temper for twenty years.' Time stood still and I'm sure he expected me to spin around and skewer him with the meat thermometer for daring to say that. But instead my first thought was, 'Oh, my God! Can that be true? Is this another blind spot in my life?' And I ran back to my room to ask the Lord about it. The Lord said, 'Yeah, it's true', and I repented and asked him to undo any damage I'd done to my family and thanked him for showing me before it was too late. (Twenty years was not too late, apparently. What would have been? Twenty years and one day, I suppose, if I had not repented.) It was getting late and I didn't want to be late for the meeting, so I hurried out the front door after apologising to John for my temper and kissed him goodbye. I didn't realise at the time what a revolutionary event that was for him: Carol apologising, instead of getting hurt or angry! Wow! Talk about a sign and wonder!

He told me that after I had left for the meeting, he got up and went back to the bedroom, threw himself across the bed and asked the Lord, 'What's wrong with me, Lord? I can see you've really changed Carol. What's wrong with me?' The Holy Spirit struck him like lightening and he cried and spoke in tongues and prayed for hours. He didn't tell me about it right away, either, possibly remembering what happened the last time that he told me.

But he was healed! That gaping wound in his spirit was healed. It's funny to think about it now. There I was, having had this experience with God and not telling John about it because I didn't want to influence him. There was John having had this experience with God and not telling me about it, for whatever reason. I kept my mouth shut almost perfectly, except for one occasion when I asked permission just to right a wrong perception that John had about me. I thought the Lord gave me permission, so I said to John over breakfast one morning, 'John,' I said, trying to sound casual with my heart beating double-time, 'if you ever decide to pastor a church again. I just want you to know, I'm with you all the way.' He slowly laid the paper down, after removing his glasses, and turned and gave me a long level look – like 'I'm going to have her committed'. In retrospect, I don't think it was the Lord that gave me permission to speak. I think I just wanted to hurry things along. Nevertheless, John became an intricate part of the meetings, the 'Afterglow'. I don't think there was ever any doubt that he was the pastor. He had always been the pastor, even when he wasn't there. As an absent parent is still the parent. During this whole time, he was never gone on a weekend, so he never missed a meeting.

People who had left or had fallen away when John left started coming back, and the meeting continued to grow along with the Lord's presence. Whatever was being said about us, it was not a Charismatic meeting in the popular church sense of the word. Brokenness and a hunger for God was more the earmark than was a demonstration of the gifts. It became common for proud, cynical men to crumple in tears as they sat there on the floor in the presence of God. All the gifts were manifest, but since we were all Quakers and knew nothing about the Charismatic world, they flowed in a sweet quiet way that didn't frighten anyone.

We were having a glorious time and didn't notice that tensions were building at the church. Actually, some of us did notice but didn't want to be the big quencher by talking about it. I was the only one who knew for sure that they would ask us to leave eventually. I knew because of what God had shown me, but I wouldn't have told anyone else that, even John. Especially John! John was really such a guileless person and it didn't occur to him that we would be asked to leave. He thought the Quakers would be as happy as he was over a visitation from God. After all, hadn't we all prayed together for this for years? It was awkward because, even though John was not a pastor at the church any more, he was still on the board of Yearly Meeting and he was their consultant for church planting.

One day I commented to John that this couldn't last much longer without causing a problem. He gave me one of those clear natural prophecies that became part of the whole mix. 'We'll have our first meeting the first week in May.' This was sometime in December. I don't believe that John had fully understood, until that moment of revelation, that we would actually be asked to leave.

It wasn't long before we were asked to come to a meeting with the superintendent of Yearly Meeting. John was questioned about what was taking place at the Yorba Linda church and what part we had in it. John explained as best he could that in his opinion this was a genuine outpouring of the Holy Spirit and could be the beginning of the revival for which we had all prayed. Perhaps we could even facilitate this visitation by allowing the new church plant in Anaheim Hills to be open to the gifts of the Spirit. The superintendent of Yearly Meeting asked if there was any 'tongues-speaking' and John answered that he had not heard any but would conjecture that it was a strong possibility and, yes, there is usually a manifestation of the gifts during a spiritual outpouring. John was asked if there was any 'laying on of hands' going on, or 'casting out of demons'. It sounded fun but not like anything we were experiencing yet. (It must have been a prophecy because in just a few weeks, all that stuff was going on!)

As to his involvement, John said it was total and would remain that way. 'Can't we have the fire without the "tongues"?' the superintendent asked. 'No,' John answered. 'If this is God – and I believe it is – we are going to let him do whatever he wants to do with us.' That sort of ended that subject and they went on to the effect this would have on the denomination. 'John, you know about these things. I'm asking you as our consultant now. Can we let this go and will it die out as time goes by?' John replied that it would not die out, that, in fact, it would grow. 'Then how can we keep the status quo?' he asked John. 'If keeping things the way they have always been is what you want, then you will have to separate the ones who are departing from that value,' John answered. 'Thank you for being so truthful, John. I've talked with the elders at the Yorba Linda church and they do not want a "tongues" outbreak, so they would like you and whoever else is involved to resign your membership.' John replied that we would do whatever they wanted, but perhaps they had misunderstood what was happening. This was not about 'tongues', it was about the Holy Spirit and repentance was the earmark rather than tongues, or any of the other gifts. But this decision had already been made and we agreed to leave, with the proviso that the elders give us their blessing as we give them our resignation. Yes, the superintendent agreed, he would talk to the elders and get back to us. He needed a list of the families who were involved.

We loved these people. They were our spiritual parents and whatever good had happened to us since we had come to know Jesus, it happened through them. We wanted to do what they asked with as little pain to them as possible, so we met with the main families involved and explained that the church felt it was impossible for us to stay. We would leave and see what God would do, but, in the meantime, the church needed to know who would be leaving, so would they sign the letter resigning membership if they would not be staying with the church. That's about all we said. Very soberly, they lined up to sign the list. Some of these people were Quakers all the way back to George Fox and they were giving up their membership. It was extremely difficult for John as well as for all of us to give up the hope that this was the long-awaited revival for the Quakers.

The following Sunday night at the meeting we explained

as simply as possible that the church some of us attended was having a hard time with these meetings, so we would be starting a new work, but we were not urging anyone to come with us. We didn't even mention that Ministry and Counsel had asked us to leave because we didn't want to turn the hearts of the people attending the 'Afterglow' away from the church.

So we left, about sixty of us. Probably twenty or so adults and the rest young people, all sixteen to twenty-five years old. Not counting our children – or cattle – we started off for the promised land.

John and I went up to the mountains the following week to pray and think about what we should do. We had become friends with Don McClure who pastored the Calvary Chapel at Twin Peaks, and we sometimes visited that church. John loved the worship and Don was a fine teacher. We had kept him informed about the situation with our church and we shared with him the events of the last week. He asked us what we were going to do and we told him the truth. We didn't know. It was at that point that he suggested something we had never thought – we could become a Calvary Chapel! We didn't understand how this could be since we had never been a part of Calvary Chapel, nor were we out of a Calvary Chapel. He said it wasn't any problem. He would sponsor us, so to speak. It was as simple as that.

None of us believed in independent churches and we did respect the work the Calvary Chapels were doing, so we gratefully accepted his kind offer to us. We notified Ministry and Counsel that we would be joining the Calvary Chapels and they wrote us the letter of release of our membership and gave us their blessing to start a Calvary Chapel in Yorba Linda. That was it. I know it was painful for both sides. The people at the church, many whom John had brought to the Lord, thought we just left them – that it was our decision to leave. We couldn't tell them otherwise without damaging their relationship to the Quaker church, so we just kept silent and concentrated on the wonderful and glorious times we were having in the Lord.

Somewhere during these months, Peter Wagner had urged John to start a church, doing it the way it ought to be done for our generation. Maybe that's why John looked at me the way he did when I told him I was behind him if he ever wanted to pastor again. Maybe he didn't think I was crazy. Maybe it was the Lord when I said that!

John, Bob Fulton, and Carl Tuttle (the worship leader) all went up to the mountains to Twin Peaks. Don McClure laid hands on them and prayed a sweet simple prayer of blessing, and that was it! It was wonderful to us. No fancy-shmancy ceremony, just the basic laying on of hands and a prayer. We loved it! No one wore a suit, either. Just Levis from now on. Boy, it doesn't get any better than that! We were home! Yes, sir-ree.

Before we leave the subject of the Friends Church, it's notable that twenty-one years later they sing the Vineyard songs, they baptise in water, they have bread and wine communion, and it isn't a problem to them if someone is a 'tongues-speaker'. If this visitation had come twenty-one years later, we would all be a bunch of Quakers!

In downtown Yorba Linda on Main Street, there is a little two-storey building about halfway down the street that we are all very found of. It was our very first meeting place and was kindly offered to us by a member of the Masons when we had been turned down by almost every church. A friend commented to us as we were describing our dilemma, 'There's never any room at the inn.'

We had our first meeting as a new church in the first week of May, Mother's Day 1977, just as John had prophesied. What a happy time it was. We had coffee and doughnuts and worshipped for an hour with the little kids running around dancing and playing. Since we had no children's programme (we had no programmes actually), we started out with a puppet show with a Bible theme before John taught.

This particular Masonic lodge was the upstairs of the building and held about one hundred and fifty people, although there were only sixty or seventy of us that first

John and his mother, Genevieve

Carol and her youngest grandchild, Daniel

John with his half-brothers, Bill (centre) and George, on the occasion of their first visit to California after John found them

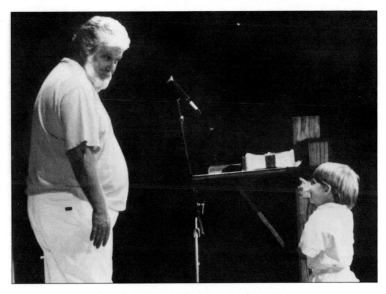

John on stage with his grandson, Evan

John and Carol in 1982

John and Carol in 1994, following the cancer treatments

The smile that everyone will remember

The Wimber family gathering after hearing about Chris's illness.
Back row: Christy, Camiline, Sean, Sharon, Tim, Nathaniel,
Carol, John, Debbie, Chris, Stephanie, Danny
Front row: Christian, Evan, Katy, Courtney (behind Katy),
Devon, Genevieve, Jesse, Sean

Sunday. Since that was the only Masonic lodge I have ever been in, I don't know if they are all alike – but this one had wonderful big dark throne-like chairs in blue velvet on the low stage area and all along the walls. Also, if I remember correctly (and I know I do – who could forget?), there was a 'G' hanging from the ceiling right over the place where John would teach.

It wasn't alarming like years later in the huge temporary tent with the whole set of hanging speakers swinging over his head during one of our awful wind storms, but it was a noticeable 'G' hanging there. I asked around and someone told me it stood for God or Geometry, perhaps both. That little mystery solved, we could listen to John.

When I remember that first meeting I always picture us as joyful and laughing. So Happy-Happy, like in *Mary Poppins* when they laughed so hilariously that they ascended up to the ceiling. Emotionally, that's what it felt like. It's odd I remember it that way, because John's first message for us was quite sobering. Since it was Mother's Day, he spoke of Mary the mother of Jesus and how she conceived by the Holy Spirit the child born to her, but all her life she was followed by rumours of immorality and her child called illegitimate, a bastard. He said it would be the same way for us and warned us not to get distracted by criticism, but to enjoy all the wonderful things that the Lord was going to teach us. (Another of those naturally supernatural prophecies.)

What has come to be synonymous with the Vineyard, the casual dress code, was certainly evident that morning. Most of them wouldn't even have worn shoes except that it was raining. Some of us sat in the chairs but just as many sat on the floor like they were used to doing at the Afterglow.

After the short but profound message was done, we worshipped some more for half an hour or so and then we all went over to the park across the street for a picnic. Maybe that was the second week. Were we crazy enough to have a picnic in the pouring down rain? Well, yes, we were crazy enough to do anything, but California rain is not like other rain. It's more like in-the-shower-kind-of-rain, and not to be trifled with. Our mountains are water-soluble out here.

Outside of my mother, John and I were the oldest people there. John was forty-three and I was forty. When the church board had sent someone to the Afterglow to count tithing units as they were preparing our ejection, they didn't even count the young people between fifteen and twenty-one who comprised two-thirds of the group. If it was a divorce, then they got the house but we got the kids. We have often said in recounting our history that at the beginning we had to use the youth for people because that's all there was. Seriously, we didn't have a youth programme. We 'were' a youth programme. We didn't even think of them as youth; these were the church with all the responsibility and privilege of the Church of Jesus Christ. When we first came to the UK in 1981, we didn't even notice until it was pointed out to us that our first 'team' was composed of teenagers. We thought of them as people. Perhaps that was a key to our success.

It was in the Masonic lodge where we were for seven weeks or so that the first 'church' healing occurred. A young man had lost his job because of a discovered birth defect in his spine. A X-ray established that his spine narrowed at the small of his back, which made it vulnerable to injury and, consequently, he would be unable to do whatever the job required. He asked the group of young people to pray for him because he really needed that job. When they did, he felt intense heat on that part of his back and when he insisted the next day that they X-ray him again, the picture showed a perfectly normal back and he kept his job!

I couldn't keep a journal at the time it was all happening because I was too excited, but I did write to Gunner regularly, so I almost have a journal. Before he died, I had written him and asked if he had kept my letters. If so, would he send them back? He did, so I can quote from some of them and you can understand better where we were at that time. (It amazes and embarrasses me to see how pseudo-spiritual I still sound, even after my 'breaking' experience.)

November 28, 1976
Gunner, a most beautiful and wonderful thing is happening in our lives ... John is fine. God is healing a
wound that has been hurting him for years. He once
again feels that approving smile shining on him. I think
the Lord has given us back that hope and expectancy
that we had at first ... for holiness, for change, for his
presence. There is a group of us that meet at Wickwires
after church on Sunday night ... It is a worship time.
We just talk about Jesus, sing to him and pray. It's really
great. We love it and it is the highlight of my week. No
one leads. Different men are asked to share some verses
or a thought from the Word, but everybody gets to
share ... I am impressed that this thing with me seems
to be lasting. It's been three or four months.

January 19, 1977
Gunner ... much more has happened here since the
first part of this letter. God has had mercy on us and
we are in the midst of a beautiful renewal. The way the
Spirit of Jesus moves on people is the most beautiful
thing I have ever experienced. It seems that somehow
God waited for John and me to be healed spiritually,
before he could move on the people here. Some sort of
invisible connection that I recognise, but don't understand ...
     Jesus had been our focus ... just worshipping him,
and it's been beautiful. It seems that in some of our
experiences we have found that we can speak a different language when we are praying ... if we want to. Of
course, this has been in a private time of worship ...
just the individual person and Jesus (no group prayer
meeting). Speaking or praying, actually worshipping in
tongues is much different than I had thought, before
all this happened. By the way, we would appreciate
you not saying anything about this yet to anyone. If the
Friends Church in America knew that John had experienced this, their ears would be closed to him and his

ministry. Boy, Gunner! John has changed so much. That hardness and distance that has characterized his life for so long is gone. He's all soft again, like when you were here. Remember?

I have never been happier. And then to see the people I love, who had been wounded or just wandered away for other reasons, come back to Jesus in such a full beautiful way . . . well, it's more than I can express.

February 16, 1977

Dear Gunner, God continues to move and it's so beautiful to be a part of it and to watch what he does. I have never seen or heard anything like this before . . . With no one person being predominant, this thing continues to grow and grow. There were over one hundred and twenty-five last Sunday night at Wickwires. We have no program, no lesson from an appointed individual, but after worship (and sometimes during), different ones will share from the scriptures . . . and all on the same theme. God's goodness and mercy and holiness and his desire to feed and nourish the hungry ones. His care of the weak and wounded. God works it all together.

No kidding, Gunner, there is a sweet heaviness that keeps control and orders the meeting. At the end we break up into small groups and pray. It's not unusual to hear sobs . . . deep sobs, during this time, as God breaks another one . . .

John is fine. He's getting healed like the rest of us. It is interesting that the earmark of what God is doing here is not the gifts (tongues, etc.) but brokenness and holiness.

John is in Kansas City tonight. He hates to travel now. For a while it was a sort of escape from the church. Gunner, John going on the church staff was a very destructive thing in his life. You probably knew that. Well anyhow, he plans to reorganise things so that he will do almost no travelling after May. He'll probably finish school at Fuller and teach more up there. We're praying about it anyhow. I know your opinion of seminaries, but John is a good teacher, and beside it's a living!

May 3, 1977

Dear Gunner, I wanted to wait until things settled down here before I wrote you. John met again with K.S. and D.B. [Yearly Meeting and Monthly Meeting] and it was plain that we must leave. Dave wanted us to and John agreed with him that it was the best way. Keith was very bewildered and hurt, needless to say . . . I know he loves and respects John and can't understand this strange thing. He was hoping that we would put aside our 'position on tongues' (his words) and compromise and blend back in the church system . . . Well, anyway, we agreed to leave peacefully and save them the agony of having to expel us. We asked Ministry and Counsel for a letter of release, with their blessings to pursue the work God has for us. They accepted our letter and responded beautifully. They prayed for us and told us to go with their blessings and prayers. They are sad, but greatly relieved for the most part. After meeting with Dave and Keith, Don McClure from Calvary Chapel, Twin Peaks, called and wanted to sponsor us as another Calvary Chapel. We didn't even know that it was possible but it was so right! So Gunner, we are now Calvary Chapel of Yorba Linda! John is the pastor and Bob Fulton and Carl too! I don't know what you know about Calvary Chapel but we have been blessed and impressed by their ministry for years. Did you read 'The Reproduceers'? All of the Calvary Chapels have come out of Costa Mesa Calvary Chapel and I believe we are the only adopted group to happen! We feel very blessed and honored. Each church is independent, by the way. They are on their own except for any help they might need. There is something very right about that!

June 22, 1977

Well, Gunner, he continues. It's still happening. They are all coming back. All the lost and wounded . . . all the strong and healthy. All of them. Everyone is being touched. I have never experienced anything like this movement of the Spirit of God in all the 14 years of being a Christian.

I wish I could make you understand . . . the knowing . . . the rightness. Do you remember that story John shared with you when you were here last? About his early experience with God and how I convinced him it was Satanic. He became disillusioned at that time . . . felt God didn't love him – didn't feel Jesus's face shining on him like he had.

This is becoming a long story, Gunner, but as God dealt with poor John and his bitterness and brought him back to that sweet relationship that they had together at first, he also began to show John what he wanted to do here in Yorba Linda.

We outgrew the Masonic lodge so we have rented Barnardo Yorba Junior High School auditorium. It's big, so we'll be able to stay for a while. John looks good and is so happy, and for him, relaxed.

A neat thing happened a few weeks ago on a Sunday night. One of our young men had just lost his job after taking a physical examination because he was born with a spinal deformity. A narrowing of the spine that made his back weak and easily hurt, in fact it hurt a lot of the time. Anyway, at the end of our service we break up into groups and pray. His group had all young people and he shared his problem with them and they laid hands on him and prayed that Jesus would heal him. Larry said that he felt a hot pain come on his lower back and he bent over and he felt something move and he knew he was healed and went around telling everyone. And he was healed, too! He went back to the doctor the next morning and demanded that they take new x-rays. They did and his spine was normal! He got his job back! Isn't that nice?

I quit writing to Gunner about that time. God knows it wasn't from lack of passion! (And I thought I was restraining myself from saying anything too emotional!) It was because of lack of words to convey to him that this indeed was God. Even reading it now, twenty-two years later, I almost slip over to Ministry and Counsel's side.

I knew even then as I was trying my hardest to make Gunner understand, this was surely a situation where 'you had to be there'.

5

The Glory Years 1977–1981

Oh, the days of wine and roses, when nothing could go wrong because God was on our side and he fought for us on every front. He was right there 'to slay our foes and heal our woes' and we suffered just the right amount of persecution to keep us aware that the Spirit of glory and of God rests upon us (1 Peter 4:14).

How wonderful it was to be swept up in a move of God, in an outpouring of the Holy Spirit! When I stop to realise just exactly what we've been privileged to be a part of, it is more than my simple being can handle. The only proper response is worship.

I told you about our first church healing, but I forgot to tell you what John's response was when Penny Fulton came bouncing up to him with the good news. 'Larry's healed! Larry's healed, John! And he got his job back!' With a happy grin on his face, he replied, 'We're in trouble now, Pen!'

I'm telling you, the man was prophetic. That same week, the pastor of a store-front, fledgling Baptist church a few miles away printed up some flyers to hand out (like WANTED posters), saying that John Wimber had been expelled from the Friends Church for 'gross immorality'. We heard about it, but we were having such a wonderful time that it seemed a shame to stop what we were doing with Jesus, to give attention to what the devil was stirring up. We filed it under Matthew 5:11–12 'Blessed are you when people insult you, persecute you and falsely say all kinds of evil against you because of me. Rejoice and be glad, because great is your reward in heaven, for in the same way they persecuted the prophets who were before you' not really understanding then, how very often we would need to use that file.

Shortly before this young man was healed at church, the healings had started in the Bible study, but only through John, and after considering the situation for a while, he didn't like it that way. He was a committed believer in the Ephesians 4:11–13 text:

> It was he who gave some to be apostles, some to be prophets, some to be evangelists, and some to be pastors and teachers, to prepare God's people for works of service, so that the body of Christ may be built up until we all reach unity in the faith and in the knowledge of the Son of God and become mature, attaining to the fullness of Christ.

He asked me, 'Carol, should I get a tent? Or should I train the church to do the work of the church?' I, of course, agreed with him that training the church was the way to go, so he planned a Sunday night service to anoint the elders and anyone else who wanted to minister to the sick. The text he used, or meant to use, was the anointing of Aaron and his sons for ministry, out of the Book of Exodus, which would have gone quite well with the purpose of that service. In the confusion of that moment, as almost everyone came forward to be anointed with the salad oil I had brought (didn't have any 'holy' oil), John opened to the wrong Scripture and read it anyhow, even though it pertained to the cleansing from leprosy. By the time he realised he was in Leviticus instead of Exodus, it was too late to turn back. He anointed the ear lobes of our right ears and the thumbs of our right hands and the big toes of our right feet, and I know that any of us that had leprosy were healed right there on the spot. John and I were probably the only ones realising the mistake in references and everyone else left that night to do the work of the church with a new confidence born in the first and last Vineyard Anointing Ceremony.

Every time we began to take ourselves seriously, something like that would happen.

John, convinced now that as a pastor and teacher, he was to train the church to do the works of service, would teach the Scriptures as if they were our instruction manuals. He talked about the Word and works. How we need to be Word-workers. Not just the Word. Not only the works, but also the Word and the works. He held up a menu from a restaurant. 'This is the menu. It is not the meal.' He held up his Bible. 'This is the menu. It describes the meal. It is not the meal.' He went on, 'You know about the meal from the menu, but you must order and eat before the transaction is complete! Don't be satisfied with just studying the menu!' Very simple and profound illustrations. It is my opinion that one of John's greatest gifts was communication. Taking the profound and putting it in simple language was really his thing. Not growing up in any kind of church (an American pagan he called himself) gave him a fresh viewpoint of the Scriptures. He didn't have any areas of settled unbelief when reading through the Bible and that freshness stuck with him the rest of his life. He was always studying to find the way that Jesus did it and how he wanted us, the church, to go about it. 'It's not enough to be biblically literate, we must be biblically obedient also.'

That point was driven home to him personally one evening after the Bible study. We were standing in the kitchen at home discussing what had happened for the last few weeks. John had taught the lesson and, coincidentally, the ministry needs afterward had to do with just what he had taught. We must have been going through Acts. He taught on Pentecost, and afterwards some people asked for prayer who had never been filled with the Holy Spirit. Quite a large group, in fact, and as John prayed for them it was like a blast of lightning hit them and they either fell down and out, or they burst out in tongues. It was amazing to us little ex-Quakers, who had never seen that. The following week in the Scripture brought us to the lame man that was healed. Gigi asked for prayer because of an automobile injury when she was a child, which had stimulated her right leg into abnormally fast growth. It was an inch and a half longer than her normal leg. John, always playing around, asked her if she wouldn't rather have her normal leg grow to fit the abnormally long one. She thought that was a fine idea because she wasn't very tall as it was. John had her sit on a chair and he sort of squatted down in front of her with the rest of the group gathered in real close to see what would happen. He took hold of her normal leg and before he had a chance to pray anything, a jolt of something that felt like electricity shot down his arm. Her leg snapped with a sharp jerk as everyone gasped and we all asked, 'What happened? What happened?' Gigi, of course, knew exactly what had happened and she went home to show her family. She spent the next few days lengthening her Levis to fit her newly lengthened leg! Her mother came to church with her the very next Sunday and didn't need to be convinced that Jesus lives, that he is good and he is powerful.

So, after that Bible study, John and I were going over the events of the last few weeks and looking for the common denominator. It finally hit him. He read the story, the WORD, from the Scriptures, THEN God did the WORKS! 'Do you see it, Carol? We teach the Word, then God does the work. Like, TELL and SHOW or SHOW and TELL! I think I get it!' He was standing at the refrigerator with the door open having just poured a glass of milk. As he said that to me, the Spirit of God fell on him so quickly that his knees buckled and the milk went flying up. He managed to grab onto the counter to stop his fall. He looked up at me with an expression of profound wonder and amazement. 'I think we're on to something here, Carol Kay!'

He has told the story so often about the vision of the honeycomb that I don't know if I need to repeat it. Perhaps I don't. But then again, it bears repeating. It is interesting that every few years a leader in the Vineyard will have the same vision without ever knowing about John's vision all those years ago.

It happened after one of John's first healing experiences.

He had been called to the home of a couple who had just started coming to church, because she was very ill with a fever and couldn't get out of bed. In John's mind, he was making a routine sick call and so he was startled when the husband asked him to come back to the room and pray for his wife to be healed. John said his first thought was, 'Oh, God! He believed what I taught Sunday! I said you wanted to heal us! What am I going to do now? Oh, please heal her, Lord! Please, please, oh, please.' What John said aloud was, 'Why yes, I would love to pray for your wife.'

John said she looked so sick that she would have had to get better to die . . . her face beet red and her hair plastered to her head with perspiration. While he was yet praying, he turned to explain to the husband that God doesn't always heal, but he noticed that the husband was not listening. He was looking past John with a joyful expression on his face. His wife was up and making her bed and looking normal. She insisted that John stay for a cup of coffee. They both thanked him warmly as he left in a daze. He had been teaching healing as part of the Christian experience for months without much success and now he was ecstatic. 'I got one, Lord, I got one!' he said as he drove away. He said at first he thought it was a thundercloud that had appeared in the sky above him, then he saw that it wasn't a cloud at all – it was a huge honeycomb in the sky. He pulled the car off the road and watched it. It was dripping honey on all the people under the cloud and some were gathering it up in an effort to save it, while others were joyfully catching the dripping honey in their hands and eating it. The sticky substance that was so messy irritated others and they were trying to clean it off themselves. 'It's my grace, John. It's for everyone. For most, it's a blessing but for some it's a nuisance. Don't beg me for what I'm already pouring out on everyone.'

That vision was such a profound learning experience for John that it changed the way he perceived his part and God's part in the ministry of the gifts of the Spirit. From that point, John never took any responsibility nor did he take any credit for a healing. It is all God. Our part is to pray, to ask, and it is his responsibility to heal, or not.

During this time at the beginning, God started speaking to John so clearly about what he wanted to do in the meetings that it became distracting for him and he would lose his train of thought. He soldiered on anyway in his effort to deliver a good sermon, but most times God won the battle and John would just stop and say that God wanted to do something. You've probably seen him do it yourself, stop right in the middle of his lecture, turn his head to the side a little as if listening to an off-stage coach. He would remove his glasses, take a deep breath and apologise for talking so much when the Lord wanted to minister to someone. Once, when it first started happening, John said to the group of us, 'Please forgive me for preaching so badly. Hey, I'm usually good at this. You may not believe it, but I do this for a living!'

A few months ago a man came up to me and told me that he didn't know John personally, but had come to a conference at our church years ago. He was a Christian at the time, but had separated from his atheist wife and it had destroyed his son, Ryan, who was seventeen at the time. Unbeknown to the father, Ryan and his mother had also come to the conference and sat just a few rows behind the father, neither one seeing the other. Ryan's father said it was his hope just to get to meet John and shake his hand, but he knew it was impossible in that great crowd even to get close enough. He told me that a number of times John would pause in the middle of a sentence to look over to the far side of the auditorium where a few people were standing against the wall. After a while John just stopped and took off his glasses and laid them down on the podium. 'I'm sorry, folks,' he explained. 'The Lord just keeps pointing out a young man to me and I can't ignore it any longer. Son,' he said to the teenager, as Ryan's dad and twenty-five hundred other people looked over at the wall to Ryan, who had moved there earlier, possibly hoping to leave early. 'The power for healing is all over you. Reach over to that sick man next to you and pray for him. Put your hand on him and tell the disease to leave. That's right! Now speak to the disease and tell it to leave. Great! That's it! There it goes! You see how it is, son? Jesus just healed that sick man through your hands and words! Isn't that fun?' John laughed, 'So much better than just sitting and listening, isn't it?' Ryan's father said he could hardly believe it when he followed John's gaze and saw his son against the wall next to a man who looked near death. When Ryan placed his hand on the man and spoke to the sickness, the power of God struck that man like a lightning-rod and everything and everyone went flying, and in the midst of all sorts of commotion, Ryan helped the man who had been dying get up from the floor and he was well, obviously healed. John watched for a while with that happy look he always got when the Lord was doing something wonderful, and then he picked up his glasses and put them on again, continuing his lecture until the session was over. As soon as it ended, Ryan's father tried to make his way over to his son but Ryan was staring straight ahead to the front of the auditorium where John was already surrounded by people, six deep. He watched as his son made his way up to the front, his heart aching as he anticipated the disappointment the boy would feel when he couldn't get to John. He told me that just as Ryan got near, it looked as if John simply excused himself from the crowd, slipping away from them, and went to meet Ryan as he made his last few steps toward him. John placed his arm around Ryan's shoulder as he led him off to the side where they talked for at least fifteen or twenty minutes all alone. I asked Ryan's father what they had talked about and he said, 'I wanted so much to go up there with them and listen, but I didn't dare and Ryan never told me and I knew I shouldn't ask.'

That was so like John. Having heard God, he made room for him to do what he wanted to do. Healing for the soul of the boy, healing for the body of the dying man and hope for the father. So like him also, to go on to finish the job that he came to do, teach the Bible.

I know when he was done that night, he would have gone over the evening's events and considered whether he had done his job. Had he taught the whole counsel of God? Had he trained the church? When he thought about the boy and the healed man, he would have laughed in joy and pleasure, but it would never have occurred to him to think he had anything to do with those events. That was the Lord. That was Jesus doing what he does when he is there, and nothing much to do with John himself. It was sure fun to participate, though, and John said that the Lord had the right to interrupt him any time, anywhere.

He proved it again and again, as he would stop what he was doing to let the Lord heal someone. A woman with a severe allergy disorder found that out when she visited the church one Sunday night. Right in the middle of his sermon, John stopped and looked over to the left side of the stage at her and said, 'It's going to be OK, lady in the red shirt, it's only an afflicting spirit.' I don't know if that sounded like good news to her at that moment but she realised it was as John commanded the thing to get off her. She shook violently for a few seconds and the asthma lifted off her, never to return again, she told us later. Of course he continued on with the sermon as if nothing unusual had happened. That happened hundreds of times over the years and it wasn't unusual, though always delightful.

It was such a relief to let God run his church. No restrictions on what the Scriptures were saying. We were free to read them fresh and be open-minded to what they actually taught, with no worries that we were upsetting anyone. Right away we began to give the weekly offering away to the needy. When the offering basket went around, those who had, gave and those who needed, took. We had very few financial needs as a church. Neither John nor Bob took a pay cheque, having outside professions, and the Masons asked only for a token amount for weekly rent. I remember that when it came time to pay, they wouldn't take anything at all.

You know, I've waited all this time to get to this part of the story because it is unbelievably rich – God teaching us his ways and his works, only to get here and find that words fail me. Have you seen the film, *Brother Sun, Sister Moon*?

Do you recall the scene in the ruins of the happy little chapel where they worshipped? The stained-glass windows long gone and so the sun itself could shine on them – those first Franciscans. The joy, the guilelessness as they danced around barefoot with the children laughing and all the babies there with them and no one reverently silent, but everyone talking and laughing out loud, bringing their gifts to share with one another? The expectancy and the wonder of it all. The Franciscan crucifix with Jesus alive and his eyes open, and the light that filled that place with God's evident favour? That was us! We thought we were just like that!

Our very first baptism and communion was an amazing and wonderful event for us all. It was probably in late May of that first year. We used the pool in our backyard for the baptism, although we had heard that Calvary Chapel took their converts down to the ocean and dunked them right there, big waves and all. I would have liked the ocean scene, being still slightly romantic in those days, but John, ever the pragmatist, thought that it was a crazy idea when we had this nice heated pool right in our backyard. Besides that, he wasn't going to freeze his behind, standing for two hours in the ocean with sand in his underwear. I had to admit he had a point, and we settled on the pool. It was a lovely hot afternoon when all of us Quakers went under the water. It's funny the way tradition is established in a group. Many of those getting baptised that day were Quakers all the way back to George Fox and couldn't tell you, if asked, why they had such an aversion for the water. By then it was in the genes. Their forefathers had to fight for the right to hold their belief that the baptism of the Holy Spirit is the only baptism in which Jesus is interested, and they were horribly persecuted because of their refusal to do the 'water' thing. But three hundred years later it had just turned into a subject no one really understood. 'Now why is it we don't get water baptised?' some would ask every so often. What a joy and relief it was to lay that all down and just get baptised like the rest of Christendom.

Don McClure from Calvary Chapel up in the mountains

had to come down and baptise John and Bob, because neither of them had ever seen a real baptism except in the movies; and we didn't want to make any mistakes at this point, considering what it had cost us already. We didn't want to find out in a few years that it didn't take because we'd left something important out.

Don baptised them and they baptised all the rest of us. John taught on identifying in the death and resurrection of Jesus and how we are leaving the 'old man' at the bottom of the pool. It was a good teaching and very believable because the pool turned a slightly murky green because of the newly mown grass that attached itself to the feet of the faithful as they went into the water. We finished the day with our first communion service. Red wine and pitta bread, just like in the Bible. We found out later that Calvary Chapel only uses grape juice, never wine. I'm glad we didn't know we were offending them that day because it might have caused a rift right then. After fourteen years of being denied the right of every Christian to have communion, it would have wounded our tender little spirits then to have a new set of 'do-nots' placed on us. We were free as the wind and it felt wonderful.

We baptised about one hundred and twenty that day, and a few weeks later we baptised about forty more. As time went on our baptisms became exciting and, sometimes, rather dangerous events. As the presence of the Holy Spirit grew in our midst, timing became everything. The trick was to get the person under and back up before they went out under the power of the Spirit. If one waited too long and didn't have a helper standing by, there was a real possibility that a drowning could occur. Many times we watched with held breath as the person performing the baptism strained to lift the limp convert out of the water, only to have him slip away towards the deep end. Fortunately, there were always a few strong guys ready to jump in at a moment's notice and rescue the new believer. It's a good thing we settled on pools rather than the ocean. We wouldn't have stood a chance against those big waves.

Most of our baptisms were private, backyard affairs, but

in Denver they didn't have many backyard pools. The Denver Vineyard rented the community pool for their baptisms. As the neophytes floated face down, out in the Spirit, the townsfolk became alarmed and called the police to report that they were putting spells on people and drowning them, right there in downtown Denver! I'm sure it was straightened out eventually, but what fun!

Weddings were other remarkable Vineyard events. Now, Don Absure and Ed Piorek know how to do a traditional Christian wedding, but they each have the freedom to add their own little touch. In Don's case it was to lay his hand over the clasped hands of the bride and groom to pray for them. It sounds harmless, doesn't it? But the moment Don laid his hand over the happy couple's hands and asked the Lord to come and bless them, Don felt a jolt of power travel down his arm and through his hand. The groom went into some sort of manifestation where he became stiff as a board and started to breathe like he was hyperventilating. They pulled a chair up to seat him, thinking he was ill, but they couldn't bend him enough to get him in a chair, so they found a *chaise-longue* and laid him out on it with his head sort of elevated. Don went on with the ceremony and the Lord went on with the deliverance, and they both ended about the same time. The bad part of it all is that the wedding was in the back garden of the bride's family home. Her parents' home! They were all there – the whole family! It could have been worse, I guess. He didn't growl or anything like that; in fact, after it was all over and the guests were milling about, the bride's grandfather came up to Don and congratulated him on his sensitive handling of the situation. He said he used to see this all the time when he was a boy at Azusa Street.

Ed Piorek was the presiding clergyman at a wedding in a Presbyterian church that the family of the bride attended. It was quite a formal affair – as Vineyard standards go – with a large wedding party. All was going smoothly and the couple doing fine, when Ed prayed the standard 'Come Holy Spirit' prayer, asking for God's presence here and now to rest upon them all. Well, the best man toppled over like a felled redwood, flat on his back, out cold and stayed that way through the rest of the service. Ed helpfully urged the guests not to be alarmed; that when we ask the Holy Spirit to come, he often does and the young man would be just fine; not to worry. As Ed and the wedding party left the stage area, they were careful not to step on the best man. I'm thinking the guests were probably impressed by the Vineyard's courtesy. What do you think?

John loved it when those kinds of things happened. He got a kick out of God's indifference to our futile little efforts to be respectable. I've told you before, we were a young church, mostly youth, and many of the older people that eventually joined us came first because their children brought them. There was one family that amazed me with their tolerance. They let their teenage son come to our church, trusting that it would be good for him (he had given them grief), although they knew nothing about us. The Holy Spirit fell that night in a powerful way and, afterwards, we were rejoicing over the evening as we stacked the folding chairs and rolled the rugs up. I don't know who discovered the kid first, but Bob got the job of carrying him home and explaining to his parents that there was really nothing wrong with him and no, he wasn't drunk. 'Just put him to bed and he'll come out of it by morning. Very nice to meet you both.' John gave Bob all those kinds of jobs. He used to be a marine and could take it.

There were marvellous healings that occurred during those early days, so many that I couldn't possibly write them all down. There were two special ones that stuck with me because they involved babies. The first was a child that was in a desperate condition with spinal meningitis. The parents called us to come down to the hospital, but when we arrived there the medical people wouldn't allow us to go into the Intensive Care Unit to pray for her, so we had to pray through the glass. We did and Molly, her mother, has the record of the fever instantly dropping to normal the moment we prayed. The child was instantly healed and came home the next morning. It didn't even seem unusual. The other baby who was healed was the two-year-old son of a young family in our church. The dad called late one night in tears because they had been told that his baby was dying. We threw our clothes on over our pyjamas and rushed down to the hospital and were able to go right in to see the little boy. I don't remember what his condition was but his legs were swollen and he seemed to be horribly feverish. When we laid our hands on him, he was totally healed. We all cried together and John and I drove back to Yorba Linda talking about what a wonder it was that God was able to make something so beautiful out of the ashes of our lives.

Right away the Jesus songs started coming – like a stream of sweet water. 'Spirit Song':

> Oh let the Son of God enfold you with his Spirit and
>   his love.
> Let him fill your heart and satisfy your soul.
> Give him all the things that hold you and his Spirit,
>   like a dove,
> will descend upon your life and make you whole.

I call them the 'airport songs' because God gave them to John on his way to or from the airport. 'Spirit Song' came in the car driving home from the airport after a particularly gruelling trip. He wrote it on the back of an envelope with one hand, while he drove with the other. I have the old scratchy tape of John teaching 'Spirit Song' to the congregation. He sang a line and then had us repeat it after him, until we all knew it. A few weeks later he did the same with 'Praise Song':

> Son of God, this is our love song.
> Jesus, my Lord, I sing to you.
> Come now, Spirit of God,
> breathe life into these words of love.
> Angels join from above,
> as we sing our love song.

'Isn't He?' (which keeps food on my table from the royalties – thank you, Jesus) was another song written on the way to the airport, on a scrap of paper. It came the same way, all at once, words and music, but it came in a flood of gratitude for the goodness and mercy of Jesus. John was on his way to pick up an uninvited visitor who had called the house and informed our son, Tim, that he was waiting for John to pick him up. Well, poor Tim. John was not the original, but possibly the first copy of the 'kill the messenger' guy. He jumped all over Tim. 'Why didn't you tell him I didn't know he was coming?' 'Because I didn't know that, Dad,' answered a bewildered Tim. 'But I'm tired and I just got home and it's raining. I don't want to go out again, Tim! Why didn't you explain it to him?' 'Dad, I just answered the phone and said hello. The man said you were supposed to be there to pick him up and I said, "oh", and the man asked me to tell you when you came home. I said I would,' Tim explained. John grabbed his coat and left for the hour-and-a-half drive to the airport and he felt miserable. Not about having to go out when he was so tired, but because of the way he had treated Tim. He wept over it and told Jesus how wrong and how sorry he was and was just planning how he would apologise to Tim, when the car was flooded with the love of God. Overwhelmed with God's mercy, his head and heart filled with the words and music:

Isn't he beautiful? Beautiful, isn't he?
Prince of Peace, Son of God, isn't he?
Isn't he wonderful? Wonderful, isn't he?
Counselor, Almighty God, isn't he? Isn't he? Isn't he?

He taught us that sweet Jesus song the next Sunday.

It is amazing how fast the Holy Spirit-given songs go around the world. They fly on the wings of the wind. Kenn Gullikson, who has also written some lovely songs, was sitting next to us in a church in Johannesburg, and during the worship we noticed that he was frantically trying to write down the words and chord changes to the worship song that was being sung. 'Ha!' he said gleefully, 'I'm going to teach this South African song to my church, before anyone else learns it' (meaning us).

'John wrote the song,' I was able to say, while I patted him on the back in a comforting sort of way. It was one those fine moments that life hands you once in a while.

That was me, of course, John lived on a higher plane.

Since we were officially a Calvary Chapel and had never met Chuck Smith, their denominational leader, we were looking forward with anticipated delight to the pastors' retreat that year and we weren't disappointed either. What a group of exciting and slightly eccentric pastors! Hearing their stories was like listening to the Book of Acts. These ex-hippies were all between ten and fifteen years younger than we were and what a difference to what we had been used to! No suits and ties there! I doubt that any of them at that time with the exception of Chuck even owned a suit and tie! Probably had never even seen a suit and tie! We loved them all immediately and Chuck and Kay Smith were warm and welcoming to us. Tom Stipe, who didn't know us at all, came over to John, put his arm around him and laid his head on John's chest. It was really very touching, and John loved Tom from that moment on. Lonnie Frisbee, who Chuck had apparently taken under his wing again, after Lonnie's foray into the Shepherding movement, came over to John and me and, without a word or an introduction, grabbed my head between his hands and asked John, 'May I pray for your wife?' He was rather wild-looking, but I had heard the stories and knew who he was. This creature with all the hair, whose hands were planted in my hair, was one of the main players of the Jesus People Movement!

'Sure, help yourself. Pray for her!' John agreed. It's funny now, neither one of them thought to ask me, although I was honoured to have Lonnie pray on my head. He prayed that I would know the wolf when he came to our door, that God would alert me when John was in danger. It was strange, but then no stranger than everything else, and quite wonderful.

In retrospect, if his prayer 'took' so to speak, I wonder why Lonnie didn't alarm me, himself. Poor tormented Lonnie. Running, trying to hide from his shame, but always landing in the middle of a move of God, unable to escape his calling. The gifts and the call of God are without repentance, the Bible tells us. Chuck gave him permission to come to our church, or at least Lonnie told us that, and he would show up and hang around us for periods of time over the next few years. We had moved from the Masonic Lodge to Bernardo Yorba Linda Junior High School, to El Dorado High School, to Esperanza High School, and we were in Canyon High School by our anniversary in 1980. Just three years old and 'so big!' as I tell my grandson – probably fifteen hundred by then. Esperanza had as their mascot the Aztec Indian, and Canyon High had a huge wall-size Comanche (Native American) mural behind the platform. We thought of them as patron saints. Saint Comanche and Saint Aztec. We couldn't afford real saints or stained glass.

John attracted young leaders like flowers attract bees and with his knowledge of church-growth principles added to his innate wisdom and practical understanding of churches, he was able to help and encourage these mostly fatherless, young men and women. He loved them and was as generous with them as he has always been with his own children. Within minutes he would recognise something in a person that caused him to love them, before he even knew them. It was not a rational thing and he would say to me, 'You have to meet him.' 'How come?' I would ask, and he would say, 'I don't know, I just love him.'

John was like that, and I'm glad he was, because I was one of those people that he loved at first sight. He felt the same way about David Watson and Sandy Millar and Terry Virgo and David Pytches and Peter Wagner. He loved them before he really knew them. There were more, but not names you would recognise, because leadership and success had very little to do with why he loved certain people.

Now Lonnie Frisbee made him nervous; he made us all nervous, but John thought the Lord was telling him to ask

Lonnie to speak, to give his testimony on the following Sunday night, which just happened to be our third anniversary as a church. It was 11 May 1980, Mothers' Day. (I found the tape from that memorable Sunday, but when I tried to listen to it this morning it keeps going back and forth and is totally illegible. Just as well, perhaps. Surely once was enough in anyone's life.)

John opened the service, saying only a few words about Lonnie being used in the Jesus People Movement and then he introduced him, but stayed up there on the platform behind his keyboard the whole time Lonnie spoke. Within reach, should anything goofy occur.

He was articulate and profound and funny and John's fears were put to rest as he enjoyed Lonnie along with everyone else. That is, until the end. After the hilarious applause, John, full of good cheer, made a move to get up from the keyboard to take the mike and close the meeting. He wasn't fast enough. While John was yet planning the closing words, Lonnie was asking everyone under twenty-five to come forward. Since that was almost the total congregation, everyone just sort of crowded forward until you couldn't squeeze in sideways. Then he did his favourite and famous prophecy invitation: 'The church has for years grieved the Holy Spirit.' (Pregnant pause.) 'But he's getting over it!' (Shouting now.) 'Come, Holy Spirit!'

I read somewhere lately a supposedly eyewitness account that claimed: 'The young evangelist was shouting "More, Lord, more" and "Jesus is Lord".' I was right there and I'm here to tell you that *everyone* there was shouting and you couldn't hear anything but the roar of the crowd, as hundreds were filled with the Holy Spirit at the same time and were shouting out loud in tongues. The chairs were falling over and the people were falling on top of the fallen chairs. The leaders that could still function were shouting at one another and it was complete pandemonium. Others were shouting that they were getting out of here. Young Tim Pfeiffer fell face down, pulling the microphone down under him, and if we had ever entertained the thought of keeping any kind of reputation of respectability, it went up to the ceiling of the gymnasium along with Tim's voice – as he shouted uncontrollably in tongues with the volume turned all the way up because someone had crashed into the sound-board.

John was paralysed, caught in mid-motion as he reached for the mike, and I couldn't tell if that look on his face was profound wonder or sheer terror. Others and myself started wading through the fallen bodies assessing the situation. I met John somewhere in the pile and I told him I thought it was the Lord. After all, hadn't we been praying for power for ministry? This, John, was it! He gazed at me with a sort of stunned, faraway expression.

John's senses were still functioning, though, no matter how deeply in shock he was, because he heard very clearly the Bibles slam shut and saw just as clearly those same people stomp furiously out of the gym, some never to be seen by us again. I know we repopulated the Friends Church with horrified ex-Vineyard members. That's fine. It's only fair.

He didn't sleep that night at all. He stayed up with his books on church history and revivals and studied and prayed. About five in the morning, Tommy Stipe called from Denver. 'I don't know what's going on there, John, but the Lord woke me and told me to call and tell you that it's him. Does that make sense?' God bless Tom Stipe!

When John came down to Wagner House (our offices) the next morning, there was a contingency of unhappy staff members waiting for him. He met first of all with the associate and his wife, and I'll never forget what he said. He listened to their complaints (legitimate complaints: they'd been up all night too), until they were through, and then he removed his glasses and leaned forward and spoke very softly, but very clearly. 'I understand how you feel. What happened last night may result in people leaving, but there is something you need to understand about me if we are to continue to work together. If ever there is a choice between the smart thing to do and the move of the Holy Spirit, I will always land on the side of the Spirit. You need to know that.' It was a defining moment in the Vineyard and it's etched indelibly in my memory.

Our church was somewhat altered by that outpouring of the Spirit. As I said, we never again saw many of the people that stormed out that night, but a revival broke out among the young people and they took it to the school campuses in the area, and Bible studies started popping up all over the place. Attendance grew along with the conversions and we probably hit two thousand about that time.

You know, for the sake of simplicity, it would be easier to say that the power came with Lonnie, but the truth is that the power of the Holy Spirit was breaking out in all the groups, even before Lonnie came to the church. Certainly not on such a widespread scale, though. I think that it was just that he knew what to do when the Spirit was there and most of us didn't. After I met him a few years before at the pastors' retreat, I had gone down to the beach area near Calvary Chapel, just to go to a Bible study he was teaching, but there was no particular presence of God. He ministered in a vague sort of way to a few people, but nothing much was happening then. In reality, he walked into a move of God here in Yorba Linda and had the faith or moxie or know-how to move with it. He could 'see' the Spirit on people, but he didn't bring the Holy Spirit with him. Do you understand what I'm trying to say?

John McClure, a Vineyard pastor and close friend of ours, was impressed by the Lord to have Lonnie come and speak at the church that John and Margie pastored. I say 'impressed' but it would be more accurate to say 'coerced'. John McClure has spiritual encounters of a third kind occasionally, and they are not to be disputed. My John had suggested to him that it would be beneficial if he had Lonnie 'speak' at his church also, but John McClure thought he might just pass on that suggestion, hating messes and all. While sitting in his jacuzzi very late one night, mulling over these issues: to have (Lonnie) or to have not, he suddenly knew someone was staring at the back of his head. Jerking around, alarmed, because of the late hour, his eyes searched the area but he couldn't see anybody there. Going back to his contemplation, he felt a shock of fear as he became convinced that someone had a rifle aimed at the back of his head from one of the windows of the half-constructed houses behind him. Slipping under the water he looked up over the edge to see if he could see the culprit, but seeing nothing, he felt foolish and sat up again. Sitting there, trying to ignore the growing certainty that he would hear the crack of the rifle any second, he heard instead the sound of a man running towards him from behind and leaping over the low fence. John, unable to move in his terror, knew the man was standing directly behind him with the gun levelled at the back of his head. Finally he swung around to confront the enemy – and it was the Lord! It wasn't a rifle. It was the eye of God. Jesus asked John if he wanted to go on where he was going or would he rather play it safe. John said he knew if he chose safety, it would have been all right with the Lord. He was simply giving John a choice.

When I hear that term, 'the eye of God', now, I have a whole different picture in my mind. The choice he made is history now and my mind rushes forward to a trip to England with John and Margie. The two of them were praying for a Jamaican woman who was blind, and she was screaming with joy and terror as God healed her instantly, and at the same time all six of the other Jamaicans in the congregation shouted and went out in the Spirit. Again, at their own church, with another blind man who had just been prayed for with little results, John said, 'Sometimes even the Lord had to pray twice', and so prayed again, and the man was instantly and completely healed.

Kenn and Joanie Gullikson and John and I had been good friends ever since we met at the second Calvary Chapel pastors' retreat. Kenn had been invited to come to the retreat after years of little contact, though he had worked for a while on Chuck's staff in the early years of the Jesus People Movement. He had left to go to Texas, I think, and he planted a couple of Jesus Chapels, or Jesus Fellowships – some name like that. He eventually came back to the Los Angeles area and planted a church and called it Vineyard (from the passage in Isaiah 27:3: 'Sing about a fruitful vineyard: I, the Lord watch over it; I water it every moment lest anyone damage it. I guard it night and day' (NASB). Kenn was a natural church-planter and had the most charming personality of anyone I have ever known, and besides that, he was very funny. We've had more hilarious fun times with Kenn and Joanie than anyone else we ever knew. As I understand it, Kenn went about the area, planting churches and then moving on, leaving a good leader in his place. It worked and there were six or seven Vineyards when we first met Kenn and, of course, more as time went on because that's what Kenn did – moved around and made churches. They were church-planting churches, too. A great bunch of guys.

Some time in 1980 or 1981, before our first team of young people, we went to England and South Africa with a team of our pastors. John and Margie McClure and Kenn and Joanie Gullikson were there, if I remember correctly. Margie kept a journal and it reads like the Book of Acts.

Kenn was with us at a church in London and, at the time, he was sort of pioneering in inner-healing issues. John, of course, was aware of that, so when a woman slid off her chair, causing a loud commotion, engulfed in a classic hissing, demonic manifestation just as John had started teaching, he turned to Kenn, who hadn't seen a demonic manifestation before, and casually said, 'Hey, Kenn, this lady needs inner healing. Could you take her to the other room and minister to her? Thanks, Buddy.' He then went on with his teaching. It took a crew to get her up and to the room and Kenn's eyebrows were an inch higher than normal as he followed them back. I don't know what John was teaching that day and nobody else did either because the other room that Kenn took her to was the glassed-front mothers' room at the back of the sanctuary. The room was designed for sound-proofing crying babies, not the screaming and howling and banging that we all heard for the next twenty minutes. The way I remember it is everyone staring straight ahead, not daring to turn around, necks stiff and hair standing on end, sure that if they did they would see Kenn flying through the air as he was being thrown from wall to wall.

John just carried on as if it was nothing and when Kenn emerged later, looking like he had been through a tornado, but leading a now calm and peacefully smiling woman by the hand, John paused to ask her kindly, 'Feeling better now?' and commented on the value of inner healing.

One unforgettable day we were at the Apostolic Faith Church in Johannesburg. A woman was there who had been blind for seventeen years (though when I got Margie's journal, she said eight), a socialite and well known in the community. Lonnie had been reading an Oral Roberts's booklet on the plane on our way to South Africa and he was sharing with the team what he had read. 'We must focus the blessing (power); that's the issue. When the blessing (power) comes we have to focus it on the disease. OK?' 'Yeah, sure,' the team agreed. So when it came time to pray for the blind woman, the team was ready as they all gathered around her. She demurely seated herself in the chair we offered and waited, clutching her purse with both hands. We all waited with her. She was waiting to be healed because the Lord had told her she would be healed one day, and we were waiting for the 'blessing' to come. She had a condition in her eyes that made them dart back and forth so quickly that they appeared to be just a blur. The power of God did come on her when we asked, and Lonnie made his way around the periphery of the group coaching us, 'Focus the blessing! Focus the blessing at her eyes!' We focused as best we could and waited to see what would happen. The first noticeable change happened ten minutes into the healing. All at once her head jerked up as her eyes found the chandelier hanging from the high ceiling above her. 'Light! I can see light!' she cried out, and we all shouted together. Another ten minutes and she was beginning to distinguish forms. She could make out the wide stripes on a shirt of one of the men. John McClure, along with the rest of us, was deliriously joyful at this point; and John McClure's smile was brighter than the chandelier above her. She pointed and shouted 'Teeth! I can see your teeth!' and threw her purse up in the air and caught it again. By now her eyes looked normal but she could not see colour. We told her we would pray again in the morning. The next morning we didn't see her and when she did finally arrive, she apologised and explained she was late because the colour came back to her sight as she walked to the meeting that morning. She had to stop and see the flowers and the bright colours in the store windows and the sky and the faces of children. We told her we would forgive her this time but not to let it happen again.

It was in the newspaper the next morning and we all had the feeling that Lonnie had called them. If we hadn't been so high over that healing, we would have been more upset with him than we were.

I called Margie this morning and she sent me the journal she had kept. I'm going to write out some excerpts from it so you can get an idea of the pace at which these things were happening.

Johannesburg, S. Africa
Oct. 12, Sunday
Attended D.O.'s church for morning service. The worship was sweet, but there was a great heaviness due to the death of one of their deacons, a young soldier. Many tears, much grief. It was hard to watch. After a rather ill timed message from an out-of-town speaker who wasn't anointed. But following that, John W. gave a sweet word of prophecy.

Sunday evening service was held in a local Baptist church, a staid traditional church whose pastor is baptized in the Spirit. Much resistance in that place. John W. taught on healing around the world. Many remarkable healings took place, such as:
Old man with heart trouble – recently hospitalized for
    coronary
Man with congenital back disease
Woman with troubled ovary – could feel it move

Man with s-shaped back
3 deaf or damaged ears – one ten mos. old, congenital
   ear defect (4 generations – great-grandfather, grandfather, father, son)
Boy with asthma

Monday, Oct 13
. . . the ministering group met for prayer that evening . . .
Healings:
Baby with pituitary – not slept all through in all life.
   Slept every night since.
Epileptic healed completely.

Tues. Oct 14
Evening session – John M.
Mt. 9:35–10:8 Healing
John and Lonnie led the healing service.
Testimonies: healed lump over ear (happened previous
day), others . . . BLIND LADY HEALINGS BEGUN: a
dear older lady had been blind for 8 yrs. With Nystagnus
– name Gillian Mitchell. After prolonged prayer, with a
group of about 30 people praying intensely in the spirit,
her sight slowly returned to the point of being able to
see facial features! She was so delighted. Began throw-
ing her purse in the air and catching it! First she saw
the light was brighter, then shadows and lights, then
distinction between people, then facial features . . . 'I
can see your teeth!'
   We learned turn God's blessing into miracle.

Wed. evening session
Kenn G.
Phil. 3 Knowing God
Following was ministry time:
Words of knowledge –
Feet (bone bruise, growth) 7 people
Headaches 4 people instant
Right ear – 1 lady

Throat 4 people instantly healed.
Bronchial asthma – man
   Lonnie called those forward who want to have many gifts for ministry. About 150 people came forward: the blind woman's sight was fully restored, a blind man from birth was healed, a woman on crutches with a short leg was healed and walked alone (shattered leg), Tanya's eye was healed, woman with bone cancer healed, a demoniac delivered, and open sore healed; kidney disease on an old man on a dialysis machine (great energy); many prayed for ministry & impartation of healing gifts. Great energy flowed and hundreds were touched deeply – couples together.

Thursday Oct. 16
Morning session John W.
Church Growth 30 att.
After – spontaneous time of repentance with many tears over the stagnation of the church today – these were all pastors who are caught up in the dead Pentecostal movement. Lonnie left sobbing. John wept. Much conviction.
Evening session John W.
Healing 350 att.
People are bringing others now with severe problems – people in wheelchairs or on crutches, blind people, emotionally scarred, deaf.
The words of knowledge:
Sinus condition (7 people)
Pain on lower back (1 lady)
Bladder condition
Sciatica (1 lady – neither Kenn, who gave the word nor the lady knew the term, a nurse in the audience interpreted it)
Pain in right hip (1 lady)
Raised birth mark on arm & healing from scars of embarrassment – a young man (no healing evident at the time)

Ears healed – too many to count. Some instant healing.
Emotional healing – many
Epilepsy (lady)
Baptism of HS and salvation

At this point John W encouraged those to come forward for Baptism of Spirit, salvation, or healing. Somewhere around 100 came forward. About 50 received the baptism through the hands of the S. Af. People – praise God! About 5 saved. A girl practically blind healed, 1 hearing problem healed, a woman with after-effects of a stroke healed, much inner healing. Great glory! The power is being transferred to the church in So. Af. Praise God.

It goes on and on like that for pages. Praying and worshipping and teaching and healing. Transferring the ministry of the gifts of the Spirit into the hands of the church there. So much I've forgotten, I remember now, reading through Margie's journal. I agree with Margie. Great glory, praise God!

That's what we were doing while the tensions continued to develop with Calvary Chapel. Some of it had to do with our undifferentiated theology on eschatology, particularly the pre-tribulation rapture. We tried to pull a Sir Thomas More, by keeping our mouths shut and not having an opinion, but that apparently was not good enough. They were very strong about the pre-tribulation rapture and made it clear that they considered anyone who did not believe an infidel. Another – and I'm sure greater thing – was all the shakin' going on. People falling was totally unacceptable and singing in the Spirit was frowned upon but when they heard that we had cast demons out of a professing Christian, that was it.

Theoretically, we didn't believe that a Christian could have a demon, either, but I ask you: did they want us to leave the demons there until the poor sucker converted to Hinduism, or what? When a demon showed up, we just cast it out, without checking baptismal records.

Don McClure tried to warn us that we were crossing lines

but we didn't know what to do. John had, on a few occasions, gone down to Costa Mesa to talk to Chuck and check with him to make sure everything was kosher, and came away assured that everything was fine.

It wasn't too much longer until John received the call 'inviting' him to meet with the Calvary leaders, and he knew better than to think that it meant that they wanted to hang out with him. Chuck said he appreciated John's worship songs, but he wanted no part of John's teaching in any of the Calvary churches. He was very clear about that. One of them succinctly expressed their problem: 'When anyone goes to a Calvary Chapel, they know what to expect. But the Yorba Linda church is different. It's like going to a McDonald's, expecting a hamburger and getting a taco instead.' (Ya' gotta' admire his communication skills!)

Chuck told John to change our name to Vineyard and he put his hand on John's shoulder and said something like, 'I want to bless you', and prayed a short dismissal prayer.

Chuck says he was surprised we quit coming to the retreats. Maybe we were overly sensitive but only a masochist would have gone back, and we honestly didn't think that they wanted or expected us to come back.

The name change had little to do with our continued direction, which had been established when we were ejected from the Quakers. We knew who we were and where we were going whatever our name happened to be in any given year. And however many times someone changed our name, it didn't change us. I'm not even arguing for the rightness of that, or saying that it's good – I'm only saying that it's the way it was.

We asked Kenn if he was sure he wanted us to take the name 'Vineyard', because no matter what happened in the future, even if he discovered one day that he didn't like us, we would never change our name again; he would have to change his. He agreed and we shook on it.

You know, it could be depressing – this book. It seems we get kicked out of another denomination at the end of every chapter and I might be depressed if it wasn't for the blessing of God on us that I was reminded of while reading Margie's journal. What the Lord did through us all was worth any discomfort and pain we experienced and I'm sorry for any trouble we caused Calvary Chapel, but what can I say? It was worth it!

It was Mothers' Day, 1982, that we officially took the name Vineyard.

6

Doing the Stuff 1981–1997

If it was a Broadway show, we had a 'hit' on our hands. There was that sense of accelerated speed and automatic propulsion that happens when you're caught up in a play that God wrote. Except that we were going through our parts without knowing what our next line was, until he gave it to us and we heard ourselves speak it. 'In the name of Jesus, get up and walk!' 'I command these eyes to open, these bones to straighten, these ears to hear, that spirit to leave, in the name of Jesus!'

The group of eighteen players were teens and early twenty-year-olds from the church, just ordinary kids, if you can call them ordinary; these unpretentious American young people, chewing gum and casting out demons. Searching London for hamburgers, and seeing God do miracles through them. Going to Hyde Park carrying their guitars, to worship and 'power-evangelise' (which left the theory category and became an action-verb).

'Where ya' goin'?'

'Oh, just goin' out to tell people in the park 'bout Jesus. Wanna' come?'

'Yeah, let's go power-evangelising!'

So they met an Asian man who couldn't speak any English, but that was fine because the encounter didn't require much language. 'Do you know Jesus?' Answered by a negative shaking of his head, they asked him, 'Would you like to?' and he somehow indicated that he would and the next thing he knew he was out in the Spirit and going to 'Jesus seminary' (in their words). Feeling a certain sense of responsibility for this new believer, they stuck a note either on or next to his prone body with instructions to read the Bible, and Jesus' full name printed out – 'Jesus Christ' – just in case he hadn't caught it when they introduced him.

Glenn and Bruce befriended a couple of Australians, led them to the Lord and gave them their beds that night.

Bob and Penny, with a group of about six or so kids, stopped at a little restaurant and Penny got out her guitar and they started to worship softly and continued to worship more aggressively as more people joined in. At some point, Bob jumped up on the table and preached the gospel and two men were saved. Immediately they took them upstairs to the bathroom of the owner, who happened to be a believer, and baptised them both in the tub, clothes and all.

The team reported all these happy and wonderful events to us when they came back to the hotel.

We were gathered in a basement room waiting for Eddie Gibbs to come and tell us a little about the church in Chorleywood where we would be going the next day. When he arrived and saw the team I noticed that he seemed a little uneasy and I didn't blame him at all. After all, it was his recommendation that had inspired David Pytches' invitation, and I'm sure he felt somewhat responsible for any situation that might develop.

We had a free day on our way to York and knowing this team's idea of fun and leisure was to minister in the power of the Holy Spirit, we had accepted the invitation to Chorleywood.

Eddie talked a while about the differences in cultures and, in a cautioning sort of way, warned us that the English don't respond quite as exuberantly as we might be used to and are liable to be a bit put off by some of the more sensational things that had happened around us, so we might possibly consider toning things down a bit.

They just stared at Eddie until John thanked him and he left.

'What's he saying, John?'

'John, what did he mean, "tone things down"?'

'Well, guys,' John explained, 'we need to understand that we are going into someone else's church. We can't expect to do things the way we do at home. We don't want to frighten the people. Just consider what Eddie said and try to be thoughtful of our hosts. OK?'

John sat there watching them for a while, as they straddled chairs or sat on the floor. After a long thoughtful gaze, he stood up and started to leave but turned around instead.

'Listen, kids. That wasn't the Lord, that was just me – what I just told you. You go in and be yourselves and listen to what Jesus tells you to do and you do that. Don't be afraid, just be obedient. That's what the Lord says.' All the worry left their faces and a big cheer of anticipation filled the room.

Those young people didn't know how to be anything other than what they were. Most of them hadn't been raised in the church and all they knew is what John told them and what they read in their New American Standard Bibles with the 'good parts' outlined by them in yellow markers. Two favourites from Matthew 10, they knew by heart:

'And as you go preach, saying, "The kingdom of heaven is at hand." Heal the sick, raise the dead, cleanse the lepers, cast out demons; freely you received, freely give.'

'And as you enter the house, give it your greeting. And if the house is worthy, let your greeting of peace come upon it; but if it is not worthy, let your greeting of peace return to you.' (Both extracts NASB)

They took these biblical instructions as currently applicable, and when they stayed in the home of church members, they brought their 'greeting', which they correctly believed to be their blessings, with them. In one house a man with a blind eye was healed; in another, a deaf man got his hearing back. There were so many 'leave your blessings with them' stories, and I can't remember all the healings that occurred in those homes as they opened their hearts and homes to our team. I wish I had written them down at the time.

The Lord picked this first team of ours. They paid their own way by selling their cars and stereo equipment and anything else they had. Danny Ruppe, who looked like everyone's idea of Jesus, with his flowing hair and beautiful eyes, received an inheritance from an uncle just in time to pay his way. His future wife, our Stephanie, was part of the group.

John's simple, but profound message was from Luke 19:33, 34 – 'Jesus Wants His Church Back'. 'As they were untying the colt, its owners asked them, "Why are you untying the colt?" They replied, "The Lord needs it." '

I think that first day at Chorleywood is public record by now, thanks to David Pytches and others who were there, but there are certain scenarios that have stayed with me.

Lonnie praying for a line of young people holding hands and the Holy Spirit going from one to the other right down the line of them . . . David's daughter coming up closer to see what was going on and John shouting out 'Gotcha!' as the Spirit engulfed her . . . 'Got too close to the lion's den, didn't you?' he laughed . . . The team (who only knew folding chairs) scrambling over the pews and even using the back of the pews as stepping stones to get to people that the Lord was healing or touching in some way . . . The woman pushing her husband in the wheelchair in which he had brought her in an hour before . . . Bob praying for the arthritic hands of someone and that person yelling out, 'I can see! I can see out of my blind eye!' and a dazed Bob going outside to lean against a wall to recover from the shock.

Such a wonderful and noisy and amazing time of God's grace. Significantly, it was Pentecost Sunday, much to the surprise and joy of our team, since we didn't keep a church calendar.

I remember wondering what that bus driver thought as the team rejoiced over every encounter they had participated in and I wonder where he is today. He heard it fresh, right from the 'horse's mouth' that night as he drove us back to the hotel. They recounted every healing, every deliverance, every filling, and they worshipped in between, thanking Jesus for what he had done. It was so beautiful. How could he have gone on without knowing Jesus after hearing them?

We went on to York, David Watson having bravely invited us, knowing nothing about us but what he had gleaned when he visited the church in the gym one night. It must have been enough and he loved John right away. It was mutual.

In all my life, I've never seen two more lovable faces than those of David Watson and John Wimber. Their faces said it all, don't you agree? Everything they were was written right there for us all to see.

I've thought a lot of these brave men – David Pytches, David Watson, Sandy Millar and other men like them – handing their churches over to us and watching and even participating as the Lord undid age-old presuppositions about how God encounters us and finding themselves as we had in realms of spiritual reality they had never even thought to pursue.

Years later, in a similar unexplainable experience with the Spirit of God, the overwhelmed psychologist cautiously asked us, 'Is my body here? I can't seem to find my body – is it here with me?'

It stays in my mind like sweet perfume; that time in York when a boy began singing in the Spirit and continued the whole hour of ministry without ever stopping. It was like incense going up to heaven, continually.

I remember David Watson and his first experience that night with healing, praying for a man that saw double, and the man was healed. The healed man was rejoicing, but it was nothing compared to what David was feeling.

So many healings, too numerous to recount even if I could remember them all, and I believe others have already written about them, so I'll leave it at that.

Wait, I just remembered some more!

The team ministered to their very first severely demonised girl that night. John took a potato-chip break after going at it for a while and motioned to Glenn Schroder to take over. I think Glenn was getting tired and in a 'No more, Mr Nice

Guy' voice he shouted to the demon, 'You're out of here!' and the demon left!

A woman's leg crippled and twisted from polio was transformed before our eyes as the power of God shook her whole body and grew and straightened her leg. A few years later she came to California to visit us at the gym and said the leg wasn't quite right yet and needed another three-quarters of an inch. 'Manufacturer's guarantee', came to mind. 'Total satisfaction, or money back!' We prayed and her leg grew again. We heard later that she got married. What a lovely thing.

I had just finished praying for the swollen and crippled knee of an elderly woman and laughed as she merrily tossed her walking stick twenty feet across the room, exclaiming 'I won't need that any more!' when Blaine came up to me and grabbed my arm.

'Hey, Carol, come and watch what's going to happen. Jesus is going to heal this blind eye. He just healed this lady's ears and now he's going to heal her eye.' She sat there in front of that ancient altar of St Michael le Belfrey and laughed out loud as her eye changed from the cloudy whiteness to sparkling clear. We stood there in front of her and watched it happen.

That's how it was. You can question every one of the team and they could tell you hundreds of different stories that I wouldn't have known about. It was happening so fast and we were all praying for different people most of the time. Afterwards when we had a chance to share with one another all that God had done that day, it was a futile effort because in our excitement we continually interrupted each other, wanting to tell what we ourselves had seen.

John and I, dragging ourselves up to our room afterwards in the early morning hours, could only weep. There were no words and no need for words. We knew it doesn't get any better than this.

We went to many churches that time and to many more on the trips to follow. The young people in our church wouldn't take jobs unless their employer understood that they could have the time off when a ministry trip was scheduled and no one would take their vacation time, saving it up for ministry trips. Some of these young people had never even been out of Southern California before this but they made friends all over the world and they developed a knowledge and love for the church worldwide.

Questioning the first team about what they had learned, I was interested to hear that many of them were relieved to see that the manifestations of the Holy Spirit are the same, no matter where on the earth we were. I think they'd been half-afraid that the shaking and laughing was a local phenomenon that only happened to us because we were weird.

The old buildings and the liturgy of some of the services amazed them. After one such service, one of the young people was overheard saying, 'Wow! That was a great prayer! Can you imagine just reeling off a prayer like that? No wonder they wrote it down!'

John took it as an opportunity to teach on the value of the whole church, explaining that our kind of church can only afford to exist because of the presence of the liturgical church.

'We can be casual and free about all sorts of things like the church calendar, for instance, because others are preserving it. If they weren't then we would probably have to do it. We're all pieces of the same puzzle and we all fit in our right place, and don't ever start thinking our piece is more important than the others just because he's working with us in a special way right now in history. All the pieces had their time, and don't forget it.'

They didn't forget it. Anyone who hung around with John for any length of time appreciated the whole church.

You know, I could go on telling stories of the wonderful way God touched people everywhere we went, but we have a lot of distance to cover still and I'll never finish before I'm done if I don't get on with John's story.

I think it was before or right after this first trip that John made the suggestion to Peter Wagner, offering to put together a lecture at the School of World Missions on the effect of the miraculous in evangelism, and Peter agreed. John's lecture was so helpful, he then proposed that they do a whole course with the material John had gathered, and they did. It was definitely an experiment for Fuller Seminary, but they gave it their blessing and the first class convened in January 1982, in the basement of a church next to the campus. They called it MC510. Missions Class 510: Signs and Wonders and Church Growth. Peter Wagner was the professor on record, but John taught the course. I asked John why he wasn't named as the teaching professor and he reminded me that he was a jazz musician, not a seminary professor, and that adjunct professor is right under janitorial work in the scale of importance.

The format was the lecture and then a clinic time. (Remember 'tell and show'?) About three hours of lecture and an optional hour of clinic that John hoped to be a vehicle for training the students to pray for others in the class – which was made up of mostly theology students, a few psychology majors and about a third older missionaries from Third World countries.

I want to quote Robert Meye, Dean of Fuller Seminary, School of Theology, at this point, so you can get an idea what happened there.

'I know of only two seminary courses, which have been famous. One was the course on dogmatics taught by Karl Barth and the other is MC510 taught by John Wimber here at Fuller.'

That statement probably wasn't in the way of a compliment. Seminaries are not usually looking for fame.

John had told me that while praying one morning, he asked the Lord just exactly what was his 'call' and the Lord had said very clearly that he was called to be a 'change agent'. From that point on he never wavered in his understanding of what he was about.

I know he changed the meaning of the word 'clinic' for everyone who had ever attended the MC510 courses and later the many Vineyard conferences that sprang from that initial course. Never had a seminary experienced such goings on! The power, the healings, the deliverances! And the training! They were all learning to do the stuff! The stuff that Jesus did. Read John 14:12 like this: 'I tell you the truth, anyone who has faith in me will do "the stuff" that I have been doing. He will do even greater "stuff" than these because I am going to the Father.' (Excuse me, please, the Fundamentalist police are at my door.)

The content of the course was eventually condensed into a book *Power Evangelism*, and that book radically changed the lives of thousands of pastors and lay people all through the church.

The school had to keep moving the course to larger rooms and finally limited the registration to accommodate the phenomenal popularity of MC510. I would visit once in a while, and I was there when three puzzled delegates from an old Pentecostal denomination sat in on a lecture and 'clinic time'. Afterwards they approached John to question him. They asked him if he had been supernaturally healed, or if God had spoken to him in an audible voice at some point in his life, or had he experienced an angelic visitation, or what.

'No, never had a visitation like that, never been miraculously healed, never heard the audible voice of God.'

'Then how do you explain the miracles or the power and authority you have?' they appealed.

'It's simple,' John answered. 'I've been reading this book!' holding up his Bible to them. 'It's all in here!'

With the advent of MC510 came all the publicity and the eyes of the world on us, and although we didn't like it, God used it, so I'm not complaining any more. I don't really know where I had come to the mistaken notion of 'private religion' anyhow. Certainly not from Jesus.

The long and short of it is that what John was teaching and doing in our own fellowship and the course at Fuller Seminary spread, like Southern California wildfire in the Santana season, to the church worldwide. And God used all the books and magazines and unwanted publicity to do it.

It was not surprising that Fuller couldn't take the heat, but it did hurt John when they called a moratorium on the course in March of 1986 pending a faculty review. Though the course had broken all enrolment records, it was causing division among the faculty, especially the School of Theology. A faculty task force was assigned and a paper eventually published stating some other issues but naming the primary objection as being the concept of 'healing clinics in academic environment'.

No kidding – that's what they said – the Bible Place is not the place to do Bible Things! The Jesus School is not the place to do Jesus Things! You figure it out.

It's history now. He took it as he always did, rolling with the punches and springing back up to his feet, to go on to the next battle – but it was beginning to show in his health and it was more of a struggle back up than a spring back up now.

He was experiencing heartache, literally. Heartache in his soul and in his body. Adding to the pain and distress, one of our children was in deep trouble and I don't care what Alcoholics Anonymous says, it's impossible to remain detached while watching your beloved son throw his life away.

While that was going on at home and at Fuller, things at the church continued to grow and prosper and we were sending teams everywhere to equip the church and to plant churches. I think of them as old soldiers now, these men and women that laboured in the same field we did, that fought in the same wars, were wounded in the same battles. Some died valiantly, with sword in hand, like Brent Rue, and others were lost for more ignoble reasons. But that's not any of my business – we all served the same King and belong to him. Every loss was another blow to John. He took it personally.

I don't know what it is like to be a leader of John's calibre and maybe it had something to do with his over-developed sense of responsibility, but he seemed to think that he should be able to fix everybody. When it came to his men and women, the ones he was responsible for, he had absolutely no sense of detachment. If he had been entrusted with the responsibility of ministering in some other leader's church and failed them by loosing on them someone who turned out to be harmful, he was in agony of soul. Which happened a few times. I guess I should be glad it was only a few times. Considering the territory we covered and the number of people involved, I'm surprised there weren't more landmines along the way.

But however few or however many, John took responsibility for them all. I wasn't much help to him in those situations, probably because I'm as bad as he was when it comes to blaming myself. Oldest child syndrome, or something worse, probably. One of these days the psychologists will figure it all out (human behaviour) and I'll be confronted with the horrible truth that we were both egomaniacs – hence our idea that we are responsible for the behaviour of others. It wouldn't surprise me, because nothing surprises me any more.

'Who knows what evil lurks in the heart of man?' (*The Shadow*, a popular radio show from around 1942). An even better authority is God when he said, 'The heart is deceitfully wicked. Who can know it?' (Paraphrase, Jeremiah 17:9).

Now to get back to John's story. The criticism began in earnest now, right along with the blessing. Running neck and neck like in a race, with the blessing pulling out ahead but the fury close and gaining on him.

It accelerated as God used John and the Vineyard more and more and the race became an obstacle course as well, as the fury increased. Books and articles and radio personalities criticised him.

He read the books or the articles that he thought had valid criticism in them, and sometimes even changed his position because of some valid criticism, but he had no patience for the professional 'church-rippers' who made their living by stirring up controversy. John wouldn't even talk to these self-proclaimed Bible experts, no matter how provoked.

He took the 'turn the other cheek' admonition more seriously than anyone I have ever known, with the possible exception of Gunner, and it worked for him. It didn't work quite so well for some of our leaders, who felt they needed to give an answer to some of these critics who believed John didn't defend himself because he was unsure of his ground.

John decided that though he wouldn't defend himself, he would make the Vineyard's position clear on a number of different issues. The first article was written in *Equipping the Saints* (Volume 2, Number 3, Summer, 1988, pp. 15–16) titled 'Why I Don't Respond to Criticism', where he explained to anyone interested about his convictions concerning how to deal with criticism and assaults.

There were, of course, the biblical admonitions to turn the other cheek, to settle a difference with a brother by going to him and working it out, and the strong awareness that our brother is never our enemy. Overriding all this was the sure knowledge that John himself would one day soon stand before Jesus and give an account of the time allotted him. On what had he spent the little energy he had? What did he use his gifts of communication for? For defending himself or equipping the church as he had been told to do? What would he give his attention to and therefore bless? The things Jesus was doing – or the things the devil was doing? Would he stop what he had been called to do and instead enter into debate with his detractors?

No, he did it the way the Lord had taught him, and it blesses me to think of that fatherless man, now basking in the approval of his heavenly Father. A good boy. He passed that test without cheating once.

He didn't care much what people thought about him and he didn't mind criticism, but he cared with everything in him what Jesus thought about him. That was the factor that determined how he lived his life and the decisions he made.

It amazes me that he could be the target of a vicious attack and still glean from the assault some seed he saw as valid criticism. At one point he called the Vineyard songwriters together and gave them all a copy of Martyn Lloyd-Jones's book *The Cross*, along with some other books and the encouragement to study the meaning of the cross in the

Scriptures. He had been accused of not making the cross central in the Vineyard and, if that was true, he wanted to correct it. He knew the worship songs were the vehicles to start. John Barnett went home and wrote 'Holy and Anointed One'. The lovely Jesus songs sprang up like daffodils in early spring: 'It's Your Blood That Cleanses Me', 'You Gave Your Body', 'At the Cross', 'The Blood of Jesus' and many, many more.

The criticism never stopped. God, always true to his word, did raise up others to defend him. Wayne Grudem, Jack Deere and many others played that part in John's life, and we thanked God for them all, every night when we prayed.

Interestingly, it wasn't just the religious leaders that were after John. A few times actual death threats would come his way – usually through some demented fanatic. When one of the more well-known church-rippers was in town doing his very unpleasant and disagreeable conferences, it wasn't safe for John to go to a restaurant after church. One time a screaming, fist-flailing devotee of that man came after John as he was sitting there with some friends eating a salad. (I say salad because that's how I want you to remember him, but he was probably eating a cheeseburger.) Like Jesus, he somehow disappeared through the crowd with the attacker screaming 'Antichrist! Antichrist!'

Another time we received a phone call from Florida from the frantic wife of a man who had just left for California to 'take out John Wimber' and some other men on his list. 'Gonna' do God a favour', and she warned us that he had a gun. They beefed up security at church for a time until John asked them to relax and give him some space. After a while, they just wouldn't tell us about any death threats that came through the church, in the belief that it could just add stress to our lives – though it wasn't too hard to figure out what was going on, when three security men accompanied every move that John made.

I think a bullet to the head would have been kinder and quicker than the constant slandering and the unending hatred that stirred up these fanatics.

In his attempt to clarify where we were theologically and

philosophically, he wrote a number of 'Position Papers', but the nipping at his heels didn't stop; it accelerated in fact. It didn't stop John, although it surely weakened him.

When God first started this thing with us, I had a feeling it would be this way. I knew from the Scriptures, of course, the promises for those who follow the Lord – they get killed. I also knew enough about church history to cause me to tremble over the possible repercussions of being in the centre of God's eye.

You know, reading back over the last few pages, I realise how hard it is for me to do this thing – write a book about John. I'm afraid it's a book about me and how it was for me. John was never afraid or even thinking about these things. I was afraid for him. It sounds like he was the poor persecuted True Believer, wringing his hands while gazing up to heaven in a saintly manner. It wasn't that way at all. There was never just one thing happening. In a book, one writes down one event at a time, but in life it's all going on at the same time, and that's my problem here.

John never worried about the criticism, never got excited or agitated over it. It was merely the other side of the coin. 'Shall I take good from the Lord and not evil?' Job asks. You can't live in the kind of blessing we existed in and not expect to be hassled by hell. It's just part of it all. We knew it and weren't particularly put off by it. I, myself, was just grateful that we were the ones 'getting it' and not the ones 'dishing it out', as had been the case in my life all those years ago. So much better to be the slandered than to be the slanderer, don't you think?

While that was happening on one plane, on another our children were getting married to wonderful mates. John was sure to invite them on the ministry trips where we had many rich times together. He instituted the 'Coming of Age Ministry Trip' for our grandchildren, in which they would accompany us on a ministry trip the year they became ten. They could choose. Here's a kind of humorous story: Nathanael, who knows how to look out for himself, had his tenth birthday eight months before his favourite cousin Evan. He was considering whether he should put off his trip with grandpa until Evan was ten also, so they could go together. The dilemma was that John had been ill and was just recovering from cancer, so Nathanael took pen in hand and wrote this letter which I have saved.

Dear Grandma,
I am ten now and I want to go on the trip to Germany with Grampa but Evan won't be ten until August. I would like to wait and go to England in August with Evan but the reason I am writing this letter is . . . What do you think the chances are that Grampa will die before August because maybe I should go to Germany now. Please write me back soon.
Love,
Nathanael Wimber

I wrote back immediately and told him that in my opinion the odds were in his favour. I thought it was a good ten-to-one that Grampa would live and a safe bet to wait until August when Evan could go.

Our children and grandchildren were the more cherished by him, I think, because of his being an only child. He was alone much of the time as a child and it made him delight all the more in his own noisy, wonderful family. Not just his children either. He claimed Danny, Debby, Sharon and Christy for his own as they entered our family, and he claimed each new grandchild as a gift given to him. If we were more involved in our children's lives than the family experts deem positive, no one complained. John was the sun around which we all orbited. He wasn't aware of it though – his vast and vital place in our lives.

We had lunch all together every Sunday after church, and as we grew numerically we grew in volume. John would leave a generous 'tip' and that was good because the waiter or waitress earned it! In our defence, we always tried to pick up the food the babies had thrown around and we apologised profusely when needed as we exited, carrying our young and restraining as best we could the three- and four-year-olds, all talking at the same time without a break (that's us adults, not the kids). We made it a point to not go to the same restaurant too many weeks in a row to sort of give them time to recover. The criteria for choosing a restaurant became their endurance power and their tolerance, rather than the quality of food.

I keep digressing and getting away from the story line here. Maybe I'm trying to avoid remembering the gradual breakdown of John's health.

I don't know what it was about John Wimber that made news reporters so interested in him. I'm sitting here now with a bunch of old newspaper clippings in my lap. The *Los Angeles Times*, dated 1 February 1972, had a big layout on John titled 'Saints Came Marchin' In for Ex-Jazzman' – whatever that was supposed to mean! The photograph shows him playing keyboard, sporting big 'mutton-chops' sideburns.

Six years later, the *Times* would do a front-page extravaganza on our church in the gym and blow the cover of a number of our people. Though the article was favourable, the photograph of us all worshipping with our arms held up was a problem to those who hadn't told their family that they were going to a Charismatic church.

Every couple of years there was more publicity. If it wasn't newspapers, it was magazines. I quit counting the number of times his face graced the cover of some magazine. Looking them over now, it's interesting to see if it was a 'fat' time or a good time. There weren't any 'thin' times after the first eight years – already the 1972 mutton-chop sideburns photo shows a little weight gain under the chin. Those sideburns sure didn't help either.

Stephanie told him once that it would be terrible if he got thin. To her, he was not fat; he was Daddish and looked just right. The only time I ever saw him thin again after our first fifteen years was when he was recovering from the cancer and he hadn't eaten for six months (except for the little cans of Ensure). He looked like a Shar-Pei puppy – that breed with all the extra skin that hangs in folds. It's cute on the dog.

The interest by the media is understandable when it concerned the years after the MC510 class at Fuller, but what was the *Los Angeles Times* doing in Yorba Linda in 1970 and 1972?

You know, it's odd. For people who liked their privacy, we sure didn't get much. We grew used to it in time, and it didn't seem important enough to hold onto if God wanted to do something else, but it's been a strange way to live. A few years later, when the Holy Spirit had fallen and God was teaching us so many new things, we wanted a little time to work these things out before the eyes and ears of the world focused on us, but it was not to be. We had complained in private to the Lord that very day. It was Sunday and that evening at the gymnasium a prophecy rang forth out of the silence and skewered us to our metal chairs: 'I have made you a market place! I gave you your reputation and I can take it away!' We never complained about it again. We knew by the tone of his voice that he meant business.

I've never known the hurt and fear of a wife whose husband is unfaithful. My only fears concerning John were for his health and that had been constant, right from the beginning. I think he was only twenty-four years old when a physical examination showed that his blood pressure was dangerously high.

'You'll never live to be twenty-seven!' was the first of a long line of dismal prognoses from the medical world.

Our son Christopher, from the time he was eighteen, had high blood pressure, too. It didn't seem to have anything to do with weight gain or weight loss. John's blood pressure wasn't affected by his weight either.

When he started to travel a lot, after he went to Fuller Evangelistic Association, I noticed that his ankles would get swollen and mapped with little broken blood vessels. He sloughed it off with, 'Oh, it's just that I stood on my feet all week teaching. It'll go away after a while when I rest.'

It never went away, but he never rested either, so I don't

know if it would have. Maybe it was his weakening heart, or maybe it was the blood pressure. It was hard to get John to the doctor, perhaps because when he did go it was always bad news.

After he lived to be twenty-seven years old, he had the idea that all the rest is borrowed time anyway and he was going to do as much as he could with the Lord in whatever time he had left. Every so often I would get frantic with worry and insist that he slow down and live a 'normal' lifestyle, but my heart wasn't in it either. Actually I believed the same thing he did – that his life was running out and he had only these few years to finish his job. I didn't fight him over it very often. Let me give you an example: when John had his first heart attack, which was three weeks before he was scheduled to go to Australia to start some churches, he asked me as he lay there in the hospital bed if I thought we should cancel. 'What do you think we should do, John?' I answered back, with an 'I-can't-believe-you' attitude, as if this man was delirious. The physician had just warned him that he mustn't travel at all the rest of the year.

'I believe it's important that we go, Carol. If I let these things (heart attacks, cancer and strokes) stop me, then I might as well go home to the Lord right now because it will never end. But if you say no, I'll call and cancel.'

Well, I believed what he said, too. I knew he was right and all I could hope for, if I had my way, were a few years more with him, but years without much meaning.

'I suppose there are body bags wherever we go so I could get you home and bury you if you die' (I was serious!). 'You're right, John, we'll go.'

We went to – as I write this I can't even remember where we were going but I remember that we were alone and it was sometime in 1994. John was still so weak from the cancer treatment that he could stand only a few minutes. Because of an airline strike, we had to stay over in Paris and board the bus to the hotel. John was much too weak to step up into the bus, though he gave it a try, leaning on me. His legs gave out and he started to slip under the bus, and, but for the kindness of strangers, he would be there still.

I remember in New Zealand, a month after the stroke in early 1995, a nice strong man stopped to assist Bob and Penny and myself as we helped John up from the sidewalk where he had thrown himself, believing he was righting a fall. His spinning brain would tell him up was down and down was up.

I can still hear the sharp crack as John – just learning to walk again – in a hotel in Perth, fell straight forward face down without even breaking the fall with his hands, because they weren't working just right either.

Do you understand why it is so laughable that his school-teachers said 'he gives up too easily'? Perhaps there was nothing that important to him before Jesus.

Those terrible times of pain and danger for him were times of adrenaline-releasing horror for me. Just remembering it makes my heart race and leaves me breathless. Now that his race is finished, I'm so proud of the way he ran it, but neither one of us could have gone another inch.

People often ask me if I enjoy travel. These are the pictures that flood my memory and I stare blankly in their faces, not knowing how I should answer. I've usually just said, 'Not much', but that doesn't really express it.

Everyone dies of something, I know. Cancer, hypertension, stroke, a bad heart or a broken heart, but never has any one man died of so many things at the same time!

He had his first heart attack in June of 1986, but had been suffering from progressively painful angina for a long time prior to it. True to form, always taking the blame, the first thing he said to me in the Intensive Care Unit at the hospital was 'I'm sorry'.

Since we had decided not to let his declining health stop us, we carried on with his commitments. It was just the beginning of the 'terror trips' for me, watching John's heroic determination to finish his job before he died. (I asked Penny once how come we never heard Job's wife's side of it.) If people had any idea of what it cost (and I don't mean money) for him to get to all those places and continue to minister, they would have given some sort of medal for valour to John. God knows and I guess he'll give him not only a medal, but also a crown.

Part of the problem was John attempting to run the three different organisations at the same time: our local church, the Association of Vineyard Churches and Vineyard Ministries International, which included John's international ministry and the men he was sending out around the world. Plus, there was the growing publishing company that John had originally started to take care of his own songs, but which had blossomed as God poured out his blessing on the Vineyard worship.

He tried to lessen the load after his heart attack by giving the responsibility of the church over to his assistant to pastor, but that plan was dropped when God sent us a warning dream that simply meant the church would not live through it. About a year and a half later another plan to name the same man national director, as we formalised the Association of Vineyard Churches, was stopped again by another warning dream. A verbal warning from Paul Cain confirmed it. It was our first introduction to Paul and the last of our relationship with the assistant. Can you blame him?

A few months later Paul flew out here and came to our house to talk to us. He said a whole lot of good, helpful things and warned us about some of the excesses (that he had seen in the Spirit) that were going on in the Vineyard. The basic content of the message was that John had a choice: to be Eli or to be Samuel. Would he be a weak, permissive father like Eli and raise unruly sons, or would he become a real father to this movement and correct and discipline and guide them? John, always sensitive to failing as a father – failing his own sons as well as failing the sons of the Vineyard – took Paul's words to heart. The clincher was when Paul said that if John did as the Lord instructed (became a real father to the church), as a 'token of appreciation' from the Lord, our son Sean would 'see a great light before his next birthday and before John addresses the Vineyard again'.

Well, now, that surely got our attention and John wept openly and thanked God for his promise. I think our national conference was in July and Sean's birthday is in August. Anyone who has a child that got away knows what John and I suffered. God's promise through Paul lifted an unbearable weight off John's heart, and it played out just the way God said it would – but as Sean has said, 'Dad, that's my story', so I'll leave it for him to tell you sometime.

In my Bible next to Isaiah 54:13, 'All your sons shall be taught by the Lord, and great will be your children's peace', I have written in faded ink, 'The promise given. February 14, 1980.' In fresher ink, next to it, is written, 'Sean home. June 1989'. He was twenty-seven.

That was our introduction to the prophetic, so you can understand why we went overboard a bit. We foolishly bought the whole lot of them as a package. Bob Jones' eccentricities were merely charming to us rather than alarming, as maybe they should have been. We took the introduction of the prophetic gifts into the Vineyard like we had taken the other demonstration of gifts. 'Eat the meat and spit out the bones', as John had said so many times. When we knew little about healing gifts, it didn't bother us to study the 'healers' of the 1940s and 1950s, even though we didn't like the model or their theology. Our theory about the prophetic was the same: we don't agree with the theology and don't much care for the model, but the Vineyard is lean in the area of the prophetic so we need to give these men a place and see what God will impart to us. Iron sharpens iron and all that. That's how we were thinking at the time.

The teaching of the main men became more of a problem to us than the non-teaching of Bob Jones. The emphasis on tomorrow, the coming revival that will usher in the last days, the emphasis on holiness as a prerequisite for giftedness, the conferring of apostolic position by claiming supernatural visitations. What would have been ideal for us is for these gifted men to come and minister in their giftedness and leave a blessing behind as they left, the blessing of the gift released and the Vineyard moving in prophecy. Nothing goes that smoothly and they had their own agenda and understanding of the way things should go, and they weren't there to just spread out the goodies and leave. They had something to say and it only seemed to us fair to let them say it, trusting that people would sort out the gold from the dross, spit out the bones, etc., etc. John shared his platform with them in the hopes that the whole church would be blessed.

In most cases that happened. I talk to people all the time that had nothing but positive experiences with the prophetic. Look at us, our son home and safe and saved! Talk to Alex and Debbie La Munyon who were unable to have children and now have two beautiful boys! Talk to Bob and Penny Fulton and countless other pastors whose whole church was tremendously blessed and encouraged by the prophetic.

Our personal experience with Paul was valuable and precious to us and I don't regret that time at all. It was worth it. When John told Paul that John needed to get back to what God had called him to – the equipping of the saints – Paul took it with grace, even if he didn't fully understand.

We had observed that in the light of these incredibly gifted men, many of the common, ordinary, garden-variety-type believers had pulled back in their own ministering to the sick, the demonised and the poor. They had come to believe that they needed to wait for the big revival, or the last days' outpouring, or to become more spiritual. A year before John died, he spoke these words to the Vineyard leaders in the UK, speaking on the theme, 'The Movement I Am Trying to Build':

> During the period of the prophetic era and on into the new renewal, our people quit starting small groups, they quit prophesying, they quit healing the sick, they quit casting out demons, because they were waiting for the Big Bang, the Big Revival, the Big Thing. They were waiting for the apostles to come into office and for things to get into the right place. I thought, 'My God! We've made an audience out of them. And they were an army!' We in effect told them, 'You can't do anything.

You aren't talented enough. You're not gifted enough. You're not holy enough. You're not prepared enough. Stand back and let somebody who is, do it!' We did it by, not so much by precept, but by example. In effect, I said, 'Time out' and it went against everything I believe in, in terms of freeing the Church to minister. You see, at one time in the Vineyard we kind of had an 'everybody can play' attitude. I would say things like, 'Well, if you know the Lord at all, get up. Let's minister. If you don't know the Lord, you soon will because when you realise that you can't do anything until the Lord moves, you'll want to know him.' So that sounded a little reckless but really all I was saying was, 'everybody can play'. Let's do it together. Everybody can worship, everybody can pray. Everybody can prophesy. Everybody can heal. Everybody can win the lost. Everybody can feed the poor, and on and on. If anything, people felt included. It wasn't so bad. My only point in saying all that is . . . I'm not defensive at all about what I've done except I sometimes think I need to explain why I've undone certain things and I've had to pull back on certain things because they were altering us, changing us from who we were and what I felt that we were called to be.

That's all there was to the 'JOHN WIMBER REJECTS PROPHETIC' idea. He never rejected the prophetic. He attempted to correct some of the doctrine of the prophetic people and was successful to one degree or another. He attempted to discipline Bob Jones, but he didn't reject the prophetic gifts. He loved and welcomed the whole spectrum of the gifts of the Holy Spirit.

It was a similar situation with the Toronto outpouring. There was never anything but gratitude to the Lord for the time of refreshing. The problem was with the focus. John felt strongly that the focus of a revival couldn't be the revival itself (or the physical manifestations that occur sometimes in the presence of the Holy Spirit). He believed that the times of outpouring are for the purpose of preaching the gospel, feeding the poor, healing the sick, casting out demons, clothing the naked and planting churches that will do the same.

We appreciated that outpouring like we appreciate the present revival in Brownsville. The difference is that we aren't responsible for what goes on in Brownsville because they are Assembly of God, and we *were* responsible for what was happening in Toronto. It was that simple. Unfortunately, the message that went out was 'VINEYARD SAYS TORONTO BLESSING FAKE!' That wasn't true. We love any and all outpourings of the Holy Spirit, but we take responsibility as to how it is pastored when the church involved is a Vineyard. Does that make sense? I thought it did, but it sure caused a big flap when we enforced it.

Something else of shattering magnitude happened in those years. Our eldest son, Christopher, was diagnosed with melanoma cancer. I know much more than I want to know about cancer now, but in those days of ignorant bliss before this happened, we didn't know enough to be afraid, as we should have been. After the surgery on Chris's back to remove the tumour, and the ensuing pronouncement of 'clean margins', we felt assured that he was all right. The debilitating and disfiguring hollow in his back where the doctor had cut away a huge margin of flesh and muscle seemed a small price to pay to remove the deadly cancer.

We believed the danger was past, that we had caught it in time. It was our understanding that if the cancer didn't come back within five years, it never would. It was May of 1990 and Chris was thirty-two. Their son, Sean, was three and Devon was just a baby.

Tim was married now to Sharon and they were producing wonderful grandchildren for us, which is understood in our family as a high and enormously important function. John initiated the 'Reward Incentive'. Five hundred dollars for the mom of every boy born. When we were up to six boys and no girls, he added an extra five hundred for any mom producing a girl. If a grandchild was sporting red hair, it was worth another five hundred. Chris and Debbie hit the jackpot with Devon. She was the first girl and with bright red hair besides! Minutes after her birth Christopher came out to the waiting-room proudly bearing this precious little gift from heaven: 'Here she is, Dad and Mom! The first one with indoor plumbing!'

John was so wonderful with his family and delighted in creating these games. When Stephanie and Danny, parents of three fine boys, found out that their fourth child was another boy, after being so positive that this last baby was the girl – long prophesied, John bought Stephanie a 'baby-changing' table because, he explained, the baby had changed from a girl to a boy. The 'baby-changing' table was a big strong pine kitchen table with six chairs that they needed with their growing family of big boys. He would look for any excuse to give things to his kids. Daniel was born and welcomed into the family, and Stephanie put away the baby girl things for her first granddaughter. John called him 'Danimal' because he growled, and none of us can imagine life without him.

Before what has become known as the 'Prophetic Era', we spent a couple of years with the Baptists: James Robinson and Jim Hilton and some other renewed Baptist leaders. They were a wonderful group of people and we had a great time with them. Then the Lord impressed on us that it was time to hang out with the Catholics. We bid the Baptists goodbye and they blessed us, and then we went to the Catholic communities. We had some precious, unforgettable times with Dave Nodar, Ralph Martin and many of the other community leaders. John and Ralph and Dave went to Poland together and it was a fruitful experience. Many beautiful and lasting works of the Lord occurred there and continue today.

Was that the 'Catholic Era' and the 'Baptist Era'? to go along with the 'Prophetic Era' and the 'Toronto Era'? I want to tell you something about John – he never thought of it that way. For John, there were not new pursuits, new directions, but only the one pursuit and the one direction.

Nothing changed for him. People talk about a 'roller-coaster ride', and the 'whip-lash effect' as he changed directions. But for him and for many of us, there was never a change of direction. Our aim was always to know Jesus and our direction was always to go where he is going. It was as simple as that for us. There were no 'eras'; there was just the constant attempt to walk with God. That is the truth. For some, it might have seemed like we went up and down, back and forth, but it didn't seem that way to us. We hardly noticed the mountains we went up or the valleys we descended or the change in the direction we were going, because we had our eyes on a pillar of fire and that's all we saw.

We had wonderful, blessed, holy times with all these different groups and we are the richer for it. When it was time to move on, we packed up and went, after taking inventory to make sure we didn't leave behind any of our essential identity. Thus, John's reviewing 'the genetic code' every few years. Does that make sense to you? I hope so.

Many things were happening simultaneously: the increasing ministry opportunities, the wonderful friends that we were making all through the whole spectrum of the church, the success of the books *Power Evangelism* and *Power Healing*; the movement was growing all over the world, and we finally bought our own building. And as sure as the sparks fly upward and man is born into trouble (like it says in Proverbs), the criticism continued to grow and John's health continued to deteriorate. I don't know if the one had any effect on the other but it sure seemed so.

The last few years of his life, John was hounded by an accusing stalker-type that fancied himself an expert on the law. He took it upon himself to accuse John of legal improprieties and would write reams of documents and hand them out at church, and anywhere else he could. When Christopher was so very ill during his chemotherapy treatments, he started bothering him, too. He wrote an open letter that he sent to church members stating that the reason our son Christopher was dying was because of the same reason

King David's son died: John had sinned. He found out where we lived and came by our house to hand John his new document. It was heartbreaking for me because after John had the stroke, it was so difficult for him to move and keep his balance. He was in terrible pain all the time. I was in the other room and didn't hear the doorbell, so John had to go down the staircase himself, very carefully, one step at a time while holding onto both sides of the banister, to answer the door. We lived in a small condo – as the man discovered – and I suspect he was disappointed, thinking he would find us wallowing in luxurious splendour in a 'mansion', giving him more fuel for his fodder.

One day shortly before John died, we received in the mail an odd sort of semi-apology from this man, admitting he was wrong about John. He said it was our own fault though, because we should have more information on public file so that these misunderstandings wouldn't happen.

That's just a sad little story that doesn't mean anything except to me, and it is an illustration of the unrelenting nature of the harassment and cruelty with which John lived. As he grew weaker, they gained strength. When John was found to have cancer, the rumours went around that it was because he had embraced the prophetic. There were, at the same time, rumours that it was because we had rejected the prophetic!

Our world, as we knew it, came to an end in the office of Dr Ken Wong. It happened after John returned from Japan, so worn out that he couldn't seem to get enough sleep. He sometimes slept for fourteen hours at a time, and it still wasn't enough. Bob and Penny and John and I went on a short golf vacation to Arizona, in the hopes that the sunshine and exercise would revive him. But he slept for the entire four days. I determined to get him to a specialist to find out why his nose wouldn't quit running, even though he was already being treated for a sinus infection. We went to Ken Wong, a godly man in our church who was an ear, nose and throat specialist. When Ken saw us in his office, he wasn't surprised because the Lord had told him in a dream what was wrong with John, and he knew right where to look with his scope. He found the tumour way up in the nasal pharynx where he knew it would be, although this particular cancer is common in the Chinese and extremely rare in Caucasians.

We asked Ken if it could be removed surgically but he explained to us that it was too near the brain and difficult to get at. It was treated with radiation, he explained. 'Oh, that's great!' we replied. 'Just radiation! Then we won't have to interrupt any ministry trips!' (Our idea was to work the treatments in while we were home between the trips – just sort of 'drop in' when it was convenient, for a little radiation.) Ken tried to ease us into reality, warning us that it didn't work quite that way. But it wasn't until the first three days of treatments at a cancer research centre that reality hit us full in the face. Penny went with us as we made the forty-minute drive, and she was there with us for the full twenty-four treatments as well as the twenty-two Proton treatments after the regular radiation. She was there with us when they made the full-front-head mask that they bolt down to the table so one can't move during the treatments. John had discovered that he was claustrophobic when they put him in the cigar-shaped tube for the MRI, but that was minor compared to the terror he experienced bolted down to that table, unable to open his mouth or move his head. He was so nauseous that he couldn't go for more than a few minutes without vomiting. At one point he asked the technician to undo him; he couldn't take it any more. The technician, who had worked there for years, stopped him, saying, 'Hold it, man. I've seen this cancer lots of times and we only get one shot at it. If you give up now, that's it. No more chances.' It was good counsel and John took it and lived through it. But just barely. Because he had been taking antibiotics prescribed by our general practitioner for the non-existent sinus infection, his body was completely defenceless against the radiation. He developed the worst case of yeast infection they had ever encountered. His mouth and throat and tongue were raw and bleeding all the time, and he couldn't even drink water after a while. He ate absolutely nothing for months and lost 110 pounds. I learned how to hook up the tubes for his intravenous feeding and how to work the IV machine. I hovered over him to make sure he didn't quit breathing when his lungs started to fill with fluid. I watched as he wasted away.

He was so horribly nauseated that the thirty-five-minute trips became hour trips, because we had to continually pull over to the side of the road so John could go into the bushes and vomit. One time we pulled over and John went staggering into the bushes. A few seconds later a transient, who apparently had been sleeping there, came darting out the other side looking back over his shoulder with disgust.

John didn't die from the cancer, although it had actually penetrated into the sinus; and he didn't die from the treatments. He lived through it and wrote the booklet *Living with Uncertainty*, declaring that it's not so bad. In retrospect, maybe it wasn't so bad – but it was about as bad as it could get at the time.

He was so brave. I was watching him one night and I asked him how it felt emotionally going through this. He told me it was as if he had been beaten up in a street fight and rolled over into a gutter to hide, and just hoped that the bullies didn't notice him there – he was just going to hide there, waiting for morning when they would be gone.

Pain pills were of no use because even the smallest dosage caused John to hallucinate and, anyway, the time came quickly when he couldn't swallow anything. The odour of food would set him off on a vomiting spell, but sometimes he would get a raging hunger for some food that he had enjoyed once. My split pea soup was his favourite soup. Upon request I made some for him but he accused me of changing the recipe and sadly pushed it away.

His beautiful thick hair grew thin and dry, and his skin hung in folds on his bony body. He became so small. John had always been bigger than life even when he wasn't overweight, but at night as I lay there next to him, watching him, I felt like I could gather him up in my arms and carry him like a child. I wanted to, God knows. His side of the bed was always lower than mine, but now my side was even with his. Sometimes, when he wasn't too nauseated, he would let me pull him over close to me and lift his heavy, handsome head onto my shoulder. I would just hold him, not moving so that he wouldn't start the vomiting again.

Eventually, he recovered his strength enough to begin drinking a canned milk-type product that is designed to have all the nutrients one needs. He hated it, of course. A person can't drink only one thing three times a day for months and not hate it, but it saved him from starvation, and I would gladly endorse the product for free if they asked me.

Stephanie has just called me and I told her where I am in the book. She told me not to forget how happy he was once he gained a little strength, because he was for the first (and only) time in his life actually skinny! Lean and mean, he thought of himself. He bought some 501s (Levis) and wore them with his ostrich-skin cowboy boots that he bought in South Africa. Hot Dang! if he wasn't Tom Mix after all!

Gary Best and the God's Country musicians sent him a big ol' ostentatious silver cowboy belt-buckle with his initials on the front, and engraved 'With Loving Wishes' on the back. He wore it while he was being a cowboy (until Stephanie hid it).

We bought the cabin in the mountains on our thirty-ninth wedding anniversary that year, 23 December 1993; and the following year of 1994 was the happiest of our whole life together. It was a glorious year of sweetness, gratitude, intimacy and joy. Soon Bob and Penny Fulton bought a cabin nearby, unable to resist our infectious happiness, and we once again picked up our regular pinochle games – although John and I never won. John figured out that it was me keeping him down and he changed card partners, so that it would be Bob and John against Penny and me. John was right. He won every time after that. Bob is an excellent card player and Penny and I didn't mind losing. Not so with John. He loved to win and he was totally childlike in his glee when he had a good hand. He would break into a rendition of 'Mr Lucky', a lounge-singer type of song that he wrote just for the pinochle games. The song made the rest of us a little nervous, since he had been singing it the evening we got the dreaded report from the pathologist on the cancer. But, undaunted, here he was a year and a half later able to sing 'Mr Lucky' again. Amazing resilience!

Jim and Laura Campbell, who had been with us since we were all new Christians together, bought a home nearby too and the six of us had happiness galore for that bright, sparkling year. John, for the first time, took an enthusiastic interest in decorating the cabin, and it looked like John in every room – warm and inviting and plain. He designed a remarkable garden, all on different levels with winding brick pathways and graceful stairs. It was beautiful, and I was once again amazed at his natural talent and his eye for balance. We loved it so much that the two of us did all the gardening work ourselves, except for the help of our grandsons when they visited.

We would spend at least half the week up there, and if it hadn't been for missing the kids and the things that needed to be done at the office, we would have stayed even longer. It was a joy for the whole family. We spent Christmas there – the whole twenty of us – and had the time of our lives in the snow. Grampa wouldn't go down the steep long hill on the sled, being too weak and skinny, but I was drafted by the boys with, 'Now, come on, Gramma, you're not that old!' (or thin, was the implication). I have a photograph of me in my fur-lined parka lying on the snow beside the overturned sled looking like a 'road-kill'. But nevertheless, it's worth a little pain and a few bruises to make memories for the grandkids.

The only shadow on that happy year was the sad discovery that his salivary glands would never function again, and that he was losing his hearing owing to the scarring in the Eustachian tubes and crusting on the eardrums from the effects of the radiation. It didn't stop him from preaching though! He went all over the world with his cans of Salivart (synthetic saliva) and made the stuff famous by referring to it as 'pig spit'. That came by way of a grandson asking him what it was. 'It's spit? Fake spit? Yuck! People spit?' 'Of course not,' John told him, 'it's pig spit.' Last week I found a can of it jammed under the car seat. A full can. It made me cry.

We sold our house in Yorba Linda to Danny and Stephanie and moved to a small condo next to the golf course, with the hope of playing golf together and getting some good exercise. We moved there in early January of 1995. John had a stroke three weeks later.

At first we didn't know what was happening to him. We were in bed upstairs and John had got up to get a drink of water. I woke up when he banged against the highboy, but he said he was all right and to go back to sleep. He hated to be fussed over but, of course, I didn't go back to sleep. A few minutes later he called me to come to him. He was sitting on the sofa holding his head which hurt horribly, he told me. He felt dizzy and his face was numb. Stupidly, I let him stop me from calling an ambulance. He was sure it was a flu going around that affects the inner ear. It was true that many people we knew had been sick with it. So he sat down on the stairs and came down them one at a time and then leaned on me as we staggered out to the car.

The hospital was only a block away and I guess that was a provision of God, since we spent so much time there over the next few years, rather than on the golf course as we had hoped. They determined that he had suffered a stroke in the cerebellum and brain stem, coming from a clot that developed in his weakened heart. A stroke in the cerebellum causes the victim to experience the sensation of spinning. The vomiting began again and so did the constant, never-ending pain and tingling down the left side of his face and body.

I couldn't believe this was happening. How much could the poor man be expected to take? It seemed too cruel to bear after the pain he had endured already. My poor John. He only got to be a cowboy for a year.

He improved a little with drugs to help with the spinning. His mind was all right, and we were so grateful for that.

When they suggested, almost insisted, that he go to a convalescent hospital for a few months, I told them 'not on their life!' He was coming home. I moved our bedroom downstairs and bought him a comfortable lounge chair. We did fine, although he did accuse me of running his bath with cold water on the left and hot water on the right side. I reasoned with him patiently, convincing him that it is impossible to do that.

He couldn't walk and he didn't (I should say wouldn't) use a bedpan or the bedside commode. Once I came back into the room to find him on his knees pushing a footstool ahead of himself to get to the bathroom.

Peter Jennings was doing a television special on new churches in America. He had come out to California to film the Vineyard in action and to interview John. John, still in the hospital, having just suffered the stroke, amazed us all by talking to Peter Jennings on the telephone. He sounded so well, in fact, that they had no idea how ill he was and asked him to allow them to fly him out to New York in a few weeks to film the interview. John accepted! I couldn't believe it. He said he thought it was an important opportunity for the Lord. I thought it would kill him.

Anyone who saw that TV special knew that John was right. He looked worn but well (sitting there in his wheelchair), so gentle and obviously in love with Jesus. He made us proud of him. What nobody could have seen was the effort it took to get him there. Christopher and Debby accompanied him because I just couldn't do it. The very thought of it made my hair stand on end. Chris was still as big and strong as a bull back then and he carried John in his arms like a baby into the plane, and up the stairs to the hotel room. He bathed and dressed and undressed him. They brushed his teeth and combed his hair and wheeled him in to meet with Peter Jennings, who until that moment had no idea that John was wheelchair-bound.

Afterwards, John spent half of that night sleeping on the floor because he had fallen out of bed and was too weak to call out to Christopher in the next room to help him. I think he just didn't want to disturb their well-earned sleep.

Balance was the issue here. Keeping his balance when his brain was telling him up was down and down was up. Every step taken required deep concentration, and John fell dozens of times. Danny put up rails along the bedroom and bathroom walls and down the hall. My sister Betty, who has a funny sense of humour, sent us a package of Velcro strips with instructions: 'Sew strips to shoulder of shirt and attach opposite strips to walls of hall and proceed slowly'. This might work, she said.

It was months before he could walk again and I blessed the inventors of the lightweight wheelchair as I tossed it in the trunk of the car and lifted it out hundreds of times. It was a joyful day at church when John preached for the first time after the stroke. He made the chrome wheelchair seem like a comfortable easy chair in the family room, as he spoke in his relaxed way to us once again.

We didn't slow down with the ministry trips either. There are wheelchair marks along the walls of some of the nicest hotels in the world. Before we knew that the footrests of the wheelchair could be removed, we scarred the doorways and walls so badly that we asked the management to send us the repair bill. They declined, stating that they were about to remodel anyway. It was in Australia that John broke his perfect nose, coming to bed without turning the light on because he didn't want to wake me.

As time went on, I decided I liked his new nose better than the way it was. It had a sort of arch to it after the fall and it lent a certain dignity to his appearance. Another instance of God working all things out for good. Things calmed down and our life went on and the future looked fairly promising to us. In fact, we were celebrating the five-year anniversary of Christopher being cancer-free. We were in our back garden that looks out onto the golf course (which was merely a pleasant view to us now that John couldn't play), and Christopher asked me to feel under his arm. He thought there was a lump there. I said I didn't feel anything and, besides, he always had swollen lymph glands ever since he had measles as a baby. It didn't mean anything and quit looking for trouble. The next day I told the oncologist the same thing, that it must be a swollen lymph node. He said no, it was the cancer. They removed all the lymph nodes under his arm and cancer cells were in most of them. We had some hope, though, in an experimental new drug that had been successful with some melanoma cancer patients.

If you are looking for something cheerful here, you are reading the wrong chapter. The only cheerful thing was the birth of Daniel, who was named Daniel Christopher as a sort of constant prayer going up, and the courageous way that Christopher handled his pain and impending death, and the merciful way God rested on us the whole time.

Christopher loved his work at VMG (Vineyard Music Group). He was overwhelmed with wonder and gratitude that God had entrusted the recording of the Vineyard worship songs to him. It was what he was born for and the favour of God rested on him in the running of the business, and in the decisions he made. Under his care, VMG grew into the successful company it is today. We all watched it flourish, rejoicing with him.

When they removed all the lymph nodes under his arm, he not only didn't stay in the hospital: he actually went back to work that afternoon. When the new drug didn't work, they tried Interferon. This made him nauseous, so he would excuse himself from his staff meeting and ask everybody to leave his office – just in time to vomit in the wastepaper can. As the multiple tumours continued to appear under the surface of his skin, he would be back at the office that afternoon after their surgical removal.

I hoped that it meant it wasn't particularly painful – all these little surgeries, but my bubble was burst when I had to have a tiny non-malignant tumour removed from a finger and it hurt like mad.

John and I and Chris and Debby drove back and forth together to Santa Monica where Chris was being treated. Debby and I sat in the back so Chris and John could talk about Chris's favourite subject: VMG. They couldn't have been happier. I do believe John and Chris had some of their best times driving back and forth to Santa Monica to the Cancer Research Center.

Christmas of 1996 was up at the cabin and precious to us all. It was especially meaningful because John blessed, literally blessed, all our grown children. He started with Christopher, saying what a privilege it was to be his father and the example of courage he was to all of us, and thanked God for him. He went on to Debby and then to Tim and Sharon and Sean and Christy and, finally, to Danny and Stephanie, blessing them. I thought to myself, 'This is what they did in the Old Testament! This is a real thing! Remember this. Remember this!' That lovely room with the fire going was as still as the dawn as we listened to him, cuddled up with one another or sitting on the floor in our pyjamas as the blessing washed over us.

Chris and Debby left early because they had a doctor's appointment, to go over results from the latest tests. The other families left except for Tim and Sharon, who were going to stay on with us for a few days.

It sounds crazy now, but we had almost convinced ourselves that Chris could go on indefinitely having these little tumours removed as they appeared, so it was a terrible shock to us all when Debby called from the hospital with the tragic news that the cancer was all through his brain. I don't remember the drive down the hill except that John offered to drive. I considered it, thinking we might be doing ourselves a favour if we went off the cliff now, but thought better of it and refused his kind offer. John still didn't have any feeling in his foot or hand and hadn't driven since the stroke.

John and I cried in each other's arms but tried to get it together before we met with Chris and Debby. Christopher explained to us that he wasn't afraid to die but wanted to live as long as he could, and so started once again the many trips back and forth to Santa Monica for radiation on different parts of his brain. Chris joked about his appearance, trying to lighten the sadness, and referred to the circular bald patterns on his head from the radiation as 'crop circles'.

He first went in for the radiation, looking strong and walking upright with a full head of thick red hair. The last time he went in for treatment, he was still on his feet, though you wouldn't have recognised him after the effects of the steroids and the massive amount of radiation.

He insisted on driving the car even with thirteen tumours in his brain, ignoring Debby's pleas, and giving us some moments to remember that I would rather forget if I could. John and I finally talked to him in private and he gave the keys to Debby, so she drove from then on. He didn't feel like he was dying, even though he knew he was, so he didn't want to talk about it. He said he knew he was dying but it was his intention to live until he died. And he did; he really did.

His brothers, first Sean and then Tim, moved back home from Colorado to be near him. It pleased him tremendously. He had hated it when they moved away from him in the first place, and he was glad that they were back where they belonged – next to him. They were *his* brothers (emphasis on *his*).

He would call me every day. 'Mom-moo! Where's Dad-dee? I need to go over some things with him.' John and I had planned out the year to be totally available to Chris at all times. John, who didn't have the energy to lift his head, somehow found the energy he needed to spend lots of time with Christopher down at VMG. Christopher never knew how weak his dad was. John cancelled almost all the ministry trips that were scheduled, except for a few that Chris insisted that he go on, and it was harder to leave than stay.

Bad news and good news become relative in these situations, as is obvious when I read back over my prayer journal during those times. I'm rejoicing that Chris had only two new tumours in his brain and I'm thanking Jesus that John's ear popped and he could actually hear again for three days in a row. We never quit praying for Chris's healing, and every so often I was sure it was going to happen – and though he wasn't healed, what did happen was that each day became a whole in itself. We didn't think about tomorrow and what might happen then. There was only today. I thought the Lord spoke to me once and promised me that Christopher wouldn't go through the agonising pain or the rages and blindness that usually goes along with brain cancer. This promise caused me greater joy than I could ever imagine.

I thought the promise was confirmed the next day when we asked the oncologist just exactly how Chris would die – the tumours being where they were. 'He would just go to sleep,' he assured us. 'Just sleep for longer and longer periods of time and finally fall into a coma.' I don't know if you can understand what good news that was to Debby, John and me. Chris was happy and relieved too when we shared the good news with him. 'You'll just sleep, Chris. That's not so bad.'

We were so relieved that we decided to take Sean and Courtney (the two ten-year-olds) on their trip, even through we had cancelled all the ministry trips. We didn't want to leave Chris though, so we talked Chris and Debby into coming and bringing Devon. Stephanie and the baby, Daniel, were there to add flavour.

So there we were. Our last photographs of Chris, with his wispy excuse for hair blowing in the mild Hawaiian breeze, pale, with deep shadows around his eyes and smiling softly in his Hawaiian shirt and lai, his arms around his treasure – his family: Debby, Sean and Devon.

John was so wonderful to all of us, planning breakfast and dinner in luxurious hotels and taking the ten-year-olds to the golf course to teach them the game. He insisted I drive him to the clothes store where he bought Hawaiian shirts, all around. He pushed himself way beyond anything he had strength for, emotionally and physically. He gave us the most pleasurable vacation we had ever experienced together.

Somewhere in late June, to our great grief and remorse, we had to face the truth that we had placed the enormous responsibility of pastoring the church on a young man who folded under the weight of it. In the desperation of John's failing health, we had made a tragic mistake, and in June it all hit the fan – as they say. We were up at the cabin when we heard the news. I was almost hysterical in my panic for the church. John took the shattering news by having a severe angina attack. I called the ambulance this time, but when they took him over to the mountain hospital emergency room, he wouldn't stay. He told them he had his own cardiologist and his own hospital at home. So we drove down the hill at 1.30 in the morning. I made him talk to me all the way so I would know he was still alive.

He had shared with me in January that he thought the Lord told him that he would die that year. I asked him if he was sure the Lord said that. He said yes, he was pretty sure. I thought what was happening at church might do it, but I knew he was determined to live until the church was safe. So we both went back to work and prayed and waited and prayed and prayed and waited. Lance Pittluck was called by the Lord to come and help us. They had lost their beautiful baby boy in March. Even now I am filled with awe how God uses the most tragic events of our life to do good. Once Lance was called, even though he couldn't come until November, we knew the church would be all right. John could fill in until then. We expected the church would go through a horrific time but, even so, much of the pressure on John was relieved with Lance's call. We knew that Lance could stand through any trial because he already had with the death of his son. John had worked for a long time to put everything in place, so that when he did die, things wouldn't fall apart. Todd Hunter was now the national director of the Association of Vineyard Churches in the USA and Bob Fulton was watching the international scene. And though the man whom John had placed as pastor blew it, Lance was on his way. The only remaining task was to find who would manage VMG after Chris died. We thought that we ourselves would try to keep things together there until God brought the right person for the job.

John Wimber: The Way It Was

It almost sounds as though John didn't have time to die, doesn't it? He went into the office every day and did the work of a pastor. He met with the staff and met with the board, although he was so deaf by now that I had to write out on a pad everything that was said. He released a church plant that had been put on hold, worked on the purchase of the VMG building, and spent hours with Chris every day. He had never been busier in his entire career as a pastor.

The last project he accomplished was to raise money for the poor. He thought he was going to be gone on the Sunday that we took the annual year's offering for the benevolence ministry, so he taped it in the office. It goes down in our history, at least, as the sweetest, most heartbreaking, loving and inspiring videotape he ever made. His voice was almost non-existent in its hoarseness and his eyes were faded and grey-looking in his weakness. He talked to his people as he had thousands of times before, reminding them how important it is to us – the Vineyard – to keep our covenant with the Lord concerning the poor. He reminded the church how they had always responded so generously to the Lord's poor, and he ended the message with the signature removal of his glasses while pushing aside the papers. 'Down through the years you've blessed me with your generosity time after time. Make me proud of you again.'

Those were the last words he ever addressed to our church. They gave so much it took care of the poor for the whole year and made it possible to purchase the VMG building, too.

The Sunday morning that they played the video, John was in the hospital having heart-bypass surgery. Though we certainly didn't plan it that way, it didn't hurt the cause. There wasn't a dry eye anywhere in the building.

As I watched that video, I remembered the day he finished the video project. I had gone up to the office to take him home and I came up behind him as he was making his way down the hall. I called 'John', but he couldn't hear me. I ran after him as he staggered his way along, leaning against the hall every few feet to steady himself. I caught up with him and, putting my arm around his waist, led him out to the car. He was so tired he fell asleep as soon as I shut the car door.

The next morning he made me get a pad of paper and take notes. He told me that he wanted Tim to have his watch and Sean his Ping golf clubs. He told me that I needed to pray for Lance every day, because 'they'll try to hurt him'. (I don't know who *they* are. Maybe the same agents who hurt John.) And he told me how much money to give to the poor.

By Tuesday, when his angiogram was scheduled, I had to take him in a wheelchair because he was too weak to walk. The angiogram showed almost complete blockage and a heart too weak and enlarged to function on only 10 per cent of the blood supply it required. They went into emergency preparation for the surgery, but John stopped them with the surprising statement that he wasn't going to have surgery. He was going home. The cardiologist tried to talk to him. They asked me to reason with him, but it wasn't until Christopher talked to him that he agreed to go through with it. John was explaining to the children why he wasn't going to have the surgery and Chris interrupted him with, 'Dad, I'm out of here in a few months and I don't have a choice. You have a choice. Who's going to take care of Debby and Sean and Devon if we're both gone? What about VMG? Who's going to run it?' John closed his eyes and the kids left to let him rest. I shut the door so I wouldn't be overheard, because I had to speak loudly for him to hear me.

'John, I love you so much and I can't think of life without you. But I know what you've gone through these last years and I'll stand up to the kids and take the heat, if you don't want to go through with this surgery.'

He had already decided to do it, because of Chris. That was 25 September 1997.

The quadruple bypass surgery was a success, I guess, but I didn't know if we would ever get John back. I'm not going to go into the hellish pain he experienced because I think you've had enough already in this last chapter. I don't want to do that to you, and to tell you the truth, I couldn't stand to talk about it. Even after a year, I wake up at night in a sweat with my heart feeling like it will pound right out of my chest, when I remember what he went through. I'll just say that he hurt, hurt really bad, and leave it there. He woke up seemingly all right and in his right mind, but as the days went on he became worse. In desperation, I finally planned a kidnap scheme because I believed he would die there if I didn't get him home. Penny and I worked it out that our sons would be there with the van at ten o'clock sharp. We would have him down at the door right then. I would take the wheelchair in with me in the morning. It's true that I hadn't slept more than a few hours that week, but I was not exaggerating his danger. He was so dehydrated that his urine was brown, and they continued to give him diuretics! They left him alone in a chair in the Intensive Care Unit the day after the surgery and he fell backwards onto the cement floor and hit his head against the doorframe as he fell with all the needles and tubes hooked up to him.

Everything went according to plan and the van was ready. The boys were ready to push any hospital official aside in our escape attempt. I didn't expect the co-operation of his doctors and, when they realised that I was taking him out of there come hell or high water, there were some frantic telephone calls back and forth to the cardiologist and surgeon. They were there in about five minutes as I was packing up his things and dressing him in his own pyjamas. When they saw what I was doing, they went ahead and signed his release. One of them even said to me that it was probably for the best.

I saved a funny message on my machine from our Tim who had come by the house to visit his dad. Julius, the home nurse, was there, but I was at the drug store picking up another case of Salivart and ordering two more cases. John was going through two or three cans a day, not knowing where the pain was coming from, and thinking it must be his throat.

The phone message went as follows: 'Uh, mom, uh – I came by to see dad and uh – is he all right? Uh – he seemed to be speaking Spanish – uh – he knew me and everything, but uh – he was asking me questions in Spanish and – uh, I didn't know what to say because I don't understand Spanish. Would you – uh – give me a call? Right away?'

As you can tell, Tim was shaken by the visit to his dad and it was truly the strangest thing I have ever heard of. The second day home he started speaking Spanish. Only Spanish, and speaking fluently. He called Julius, 'Julio', and he called us all the Spanish equivalent of our names. When I would tell him he had to take his medication, he would tell me in Spanish that he didn't understand English. It lasted about a week. It was another week before he understood that he had undergone heart surgery. Even then, once he understood that, he thought I had done the surgery.

'I don't know why Carol thought she had to do this surgery on me,' he would say to friends when they came by, showing them the long wound on his chest. 'I guess she knows what she's doing.' He was bewildered, trying to make sense of my actions.

I have in my thank you prayer journal dated 10/6/97: 'John more rational today.' That little notation was written down with intense relief and gratitude, I can tell you.

Things improved quickly after that and Julius, who spent twenty-four hours a day with John, listening to worship tapes, capitulated to the Lord.

My journal dated 10/31/97: 'Julius has somehow become a born-again Christian! He is so hungry for God. Been here a month and leaving Sunday. God keep him and bless him and his family.'

Julius stayed an extra week, I think just so he could go to church with us on Sunday. John and I prayed for him and he was powerfully filled with the Holy Spirit. I would have kept him there forever but I missed being alone with John, and Julius had another job he had to go to.

John and I went up to the mountains and had a perfect-in-every-way week together that I'll treasure in my memory for the rest of my life. We talked and prayed about so many things that week, and again he thanked God for our life together.

'It's been good, Carol – our life together. God's been good to us, hasn't he?' I told him once again how much I loved him and once again he thanked me for being his friend. As we were driving, I commented to him how different he was since the surgery. He asked me how was he different. I told him that he was so nice all the time now. Never cranky any more. He smiled at me and said, 'So smart, so late.' I told John that I appreciated him sticking around here with me and not dying yet, what with Christopher and all. He looked at me for a long time before he answered, 'I hope I can stay and help you.' But I knew then, as he said it, he didn't believe he could. We came home on Saturday so that we wouldn't miss church on Sunday. When I had parked the car in the garage, John didn't follow me into the house. After a while I went out to see what was keeping him and found him still in the car listening to a worship tape. I bent over to look in the window and he looked up at me with a big unself-conscious smile – like a child – and said, 'Isn't it beautiful, Carol? Isn't worship beautiful?' Smiling to myself at his guilelessness, I left him there in the car to enjoy the Lord.

Sunday morning while I was upstairs getting dressed, John, in the downstairs room, decided he could dress himself, and fell. I felt more than heard him hit the wall. I ran downstairs to see what had happened. He was lying on his back on the thick carpet of his dressing-room with his eyes open, but looking back and forth. I asked what had happened and if he was hurt. He said he didn't know what had happened but his shoulder hurt. I called Sean to help me get him up, as I had called him or Danny or Tim or Chris so many times before when John fell or slipped down because his legs were too weak to support him. A 'Dad Down' call. One of many, but what was different was the blood-thinning medication he'd been on since the stroke. Sean came right over and got him up. We checked out his body to see if there were bruises anywhere. His shoulder seemed to be the only painful thing, and he said he was feeling better. I told Sean to go on to church without us; that I didn't think John could manoeuvre into the car with the sore shoulder. Sean urged me to go on to church with Camie Rose and he would stay with his dad.

When we returned and hour and a half later, we met Christy and the kids at the restaurant. John was unusually quiet during lunch and I asked him if he felt all right. He said that his head hurt and he wanted some Tylenol. I was sitting next to him and noticed that he was leaning on me. The adrenaline shot through my body, and I told Sean and Christy that we needed to get him to the hospital right away. I thought he must have a concussion from the fall. They called an ambulance and took him the two blocks to the hospital, while we followed and gathered in the emergency room, waiting for them to give us a report. Debby called Danny and Stephanie who were up in the mountains. They made it home in an hour, which is almost impossible. Debby went home to get Chris, who couldn't walk any more. Tim and Sharon drove up from Mission Viejo. Debby met us there and we waited. The doctor let me go in earlier to be with him and explained to me the tests that they would do. I told the staff about the fall that morning and I kissed John, as I went back to the waiting-room so the others could go in. Christy and Sean went in and came back out so Debby could go in. She told John that she loved him and he smiled at her. 'It's nice to be loved,' John said. Debby told us that his left eye quit moving as they rolled his gurney away to do the tests. Those were the last words he spoke. 'It's nice to be loved.'

They put a ventilator down his throat because he quit breathing right then as they took him away. The X-rays showed a massive brain haemorrhage that was pushing his brain over to one side of his skull, and it had already stopped all brain function. It's the law here in California that two different neurologists had to check him for any response, and the second doctor wasn't coming in until morning. That was about two o'clock in the afternoon on Sunday. They kept the ventilator on him until eight o'clock the next morning. It seemed wrong at the time, but it did give Danny and Stephanie and Christopher, in his wheelchair, time to arrive. When my brothers and sisters and nieces and nephews and friends came, it looked like John was just sleeping, breathing deeply. His colour never looked better. They explained that when the brain dies, it causes a high fever in the body.

The neurologist finally came in and turned off the breathing machine. We asked the nurse to remove all the tubes and needles, but she said she would come back later and do it. She had some things she had to do first. We waited quietly until she left the room. We shut the door and Sean and Laura Campbell started taking out the needles and pulling out the tubes, piling them up on the table. Sean found a cloth and dipped it in some water to wipe the blood away from his mouth and nose. He combed John's hair and even trimmed his moustache. He worked over him until he was satisfied and then kissed him on the forehead and tucked the sheets in all around him. The nurse looked in and asked what we had done. We pointed to the pile of tubes and needles and she turned around and left the room. You see, we just couldn't bear, for another second, any more needles and tubes and machines anywhere near him.

I shut myself away in the hospital restroom and leaned my face against the cool wall. I felt feverish myself and I prayed. 'Oh, God, you've got to speak to me now. What will I do? How can I go on? I've got to hear from you.'

I joined the others and filled out all the papers that are necessary when someone dies, and I went with the family to a restaurant and tried to eat something. After convincing my family that I would be fine, I went home and fell in bed and actually slept.

I dreamed that I was sleeping in the upstairs bedroom of a house that was ours and, in my dream, I was awakened by the sound of John singing at the piano, as he often did in the mornings. The house was filled with sunlight and the sweet clear sound of his voice was like it had been when we were young Christians, before the cancer stole his voice. He was singing a song he used to sing often years ago. I had forgotten the words of the song until I heard him sing it in my dream.

Fix your eyes upon Jesus.
Look full in His wonderful face,
and the things of earth will grow strangely dim
In the light of his glory and grace.

In my dream I woke up to the sound of John singing and I ran down the stairs full of joy because I knew he was there and well and the last few years had all been a horrible dream. I actually woke up then, in my darkened room, as the tide of reality swept in. But it was the most amazing thing – I could still hear him singing. I was fully awake and, yet, I was hearing him sing, 'Fix your eyes upon Jesus'. It went on for about ten seconds, which is longer than you think. Then it faded away slowly. It didn't just stop all at once; it slowly faded away. I dragged myself out of bed and down the stairway. I opened my ragged, peeling old Bible to the organised Bible reading for November 17. It was from the twelfth chapter of Hebrews.

Therefore, since we are surrounded by such a great cloud of witnesses, let us throw off everything that hinders and the sin that so easily entangles, and let us run with perseverance the race marked out for us. Let us fix our eyes on Jesus, the author and perfecter of our faith, who for the joy set before him endured the cross, scorning its shame, and sat down at the right hand of the throne of God. Consider him who endured such opposition from sinful men, so that you will not grow weary and lose heart.

It was the answer to my prayer in the hospital and a lifeline to me. I grasped those instructions to my heart and I haven't let go. He kept me through the next few months as Christopher's poor ravaged body shut down gradually. (He never did 'sleep' like the doctors said he would. He was fully conscious until the last few hours of his life.)

A few weeks before John's death, Chris had got stuck in our jacuzzi and couldn't get out. It was horrible. Debby and

I hurt him trying to pull him up and by the time we pulled him out and up, he was dragging his leg almost uselessly. There were strap burns under his arms and around his body where we had pulled him up. John, who was not able to help, sat and had to watch the whole ordeal. After Chris and Debby left, I started to worry about John – how he must feel seeing his son helpless and sitting there, unable to come to his assistance. I asked him how he felt when he saw Chris, thinking it might help to talk about it. He didn't even pause to think about it. He said with a look of awe and wonder on his face, 'I see the glory of God, Carol – think about it. Think about our whole life together. When has God not glorified himself?'

I didn't really understand what he meant at the time. I'm not sure I do now, but whatever he meant he had a better thing going than I did and I wasn't going to mess with it.

I thought it would be worse for Chris after his dad died, but it wasn't. He said it made dying easier for him, knowing his dad was already there. Chris first started to lose his balance and he fell a few times down at the office. Then he started to lose strength in his legs. He determined that he needed to exercise them more to build up the muscle tissue. Finally, he couldn't move his right leg at all so he moved around the office in the wheelchair. When his right arm stopped working, he used his left arm to pull himself up. When he couldn't do that any more, Dave King, his closest friend, carried him. He lifted him from his bed to his wheelchair to his lounge chair, and Chris had his staff meetings there in the family room at his home. When he couldn't form words any more, he would point to Debby or someone else in the room who knew what he was trying to say. He would point to the CD-player up in the bookshelf and pound his chest with his left fist. He would point and that meant worship. He would point and pound and I've never observed a more moving illustration of worship. He wanted 'You Bless Me, Lord, Forever' to play again and again. When a different song would come on, he would become agitated and beat his breast and point to the CD-player until we put it on repeat and played 'You Bless Me, Lord, Forever'. We never grew tired of it either, but none of us can hear it now without breaking down in sobs.

He breathed his last with all of us right there with him in the family room, where we had moved his bed. Debby, lying down next to him, put her head on his shoulder. We sang in the Spirit over him as he left us.

Someone said once that though Christians aren't always healed, they sure die good. I have to agree. Both of these men died good, drowned in an ocean of love and peace and assurance.

John's brothers, whom he had found the year before, were there for both funerals. Maybe they understood fully for the first time what we were all about. I haven't been to that many funerals, but I believe those two, so close together that they merged into one long funeral, had to be the most wonderful, blessed funerals of all time.

In my prayer journal is written: '11/17/97 John with Jesus.'

And ten days later on Thanksgiving (which happened to be my sixtieth birthday):

11/27/97. My 60th birthday. My brother Bob gave me his music box. Such a loving and tender display of deep affection. I cried. Jesus, bless Bob and his family, Linda, Wendy and Steve and baby Steven and little Bob.

Christopher had a good day today. He can't walk any more. Lord God Almighty, don't let him be in any pain! Jesus, our painbearer – take his! Evan has stayed with me since John died and it's helped me. I'm moving in January to a house nearer the kids. Thank you, Lord, for the way you always take care of me. I love you. My brother Tim seems better.

The memorial service last Friday was wonderful. A celebration of John's life in the Lord and a time when God reminded us, the Vineyard, of what he's entrusted to us. If the devil thought he stopped the Vineyard with John's death, – it has had the very opposite effect.

On the front of the memorial service program it's written: *John Wimber, Equipper of Saints*. On the back is 2 Timothy 4:6–8 –

For I am already being poured out like a drink offering, and the time has come for my departure. I have fought the good fight, I have finished the race, I have kept the faith. Now there is in store for me the crown of righteousness, which the Lord, the righteous Judge, will award to me on that day – and not only me, but also to all who have longed for his appearing.

February 8, 1998

It's Sunday morning. Christopher died Friday late afternoon. I expected to feel some sort of relief. I'd begged God to take him home . . . to end the pain and torment and I do thank you, Lord, for hearing my prayer, but the feeling isn't relief, it's merely a deep, deep sadness. The whole long horrible struggle. The mask, the terror, the pain, his refusal to let all the surgeries and treatments and pain and sickness . . . stop him. Locked in that poor beat up tortured body. At the end struggling for the next breath and conscious the whole time. All of it that I couldn't bear to think about . . . it all crowds in now that he's safe.

For Christopher's memorial service program, Debby and I chose Job 19:25–26 – *Though my flesh it be destroyed; yet with my eyes I will see God. I know that my redeemer lives.* (Words from a Vineyard song inspired by the text in Job.)

Well, how's that for a happy ending? I know there is a happy ending but I'll have to wait a while for it. I dream of John sometimes and he is always young and strong and enjoying himself. In my dreams I am always amazed that he is really there and I touch him and smell his hair and kiss his face. But even in the dream, though content to be with me, he's always looking off to somewhere in the distance to some place and someone I can't see.

Carol Wimber's Tribute at John's Memorial Service

He did what was right in the sight of the Lord ...
2 Kings 18:3 & 22:2
And he tore down the high places ... 2 Kings 18:4 &
23:8

John would never have allowed me to compare him to a king. He had his sights set on the Servant role. That is what he was looking for. He would tell the story of the wedding at Cana of Galilee. Nobody else knew what was going on when the water was changed to wine, but the servants knew. That was the role he was after, to be a servant. Honestly, the only ambition John ever had was to come before the Father one day and hear, 'Well done thou good and faithful servant'.

What may have appeared to be a driving ambition to some people who didn't understand him, was nothing more than a sense of responsibility. He felt that God had given him something that belonged to the whole Church and he did not want to waste any time. That's what drove him. It was responsibility. He had a message that he needed to deliver.

But since John is not here, I can compare him to whoever I want! I have always thought of him – though I never told him this – I have always thought of him as being a king ... like King Hezekiah and King Josiah. The Bible says, 'He did what was right in the eyes of the Lord and he tore down the high places.' I think of the High Places, concerning John, as those places where 'religious spirits' dwelt and were served and worshipped. Like Exclusiveness.

Exclusiveness

John loved the whole church! What was it he used to say? 'From the bare feet and guitars, to the bells and the smells.' From the low church, the casual church, to the high church, the liturgical church. He loved the whole church. He *loved* it! He even liked it when he went with the class at Fuller to that snake-handling church in the hills of Arkansas! Now he didn't get real close, but he did go up to that pulpit full of squirming snakes when they invited him to give a greeting. (Eddie Gibbs, who was with him, said he would start with worms, thank you.) But no matter how weird or strange, if there was an expression of the body of Christ there – he loved it!

He also loved the Catholic church, and did what he could to show it. He loved the whole spectrum of the church but he always made it clear what the Vineyard was for, what our part in the Body of Christ was. But he didn't think of the Vineyard as anything more than one vegetable in the whole stew. He knew we were entrusted with something that was needed to provide that particular flavour, but it was nothing more than that. He had no inflated or unreal ideas about our role in the church. He knew that we were a vine that God had planted and John greatly valued what we were called to do, but he didn't think we were the only vine or even necessarily the best one. He understood that we had been entrusted with a partial reflection, a facet of the glory of God and we needed to be true to our unique calling, and that is what he fought for, and that is what he stood for, and that is what he was so unwavering about.

He was true to what God had entrusted to him every day of his life. That is why I have never been apologetic for some of the 'trips' we have taken. To me it has all been wonderful. The way we got to be there and be part of it. The way we got to experience God and each new aspect of God that we were discovering. When things got strained or a little twisted, or somebody took it beyond the boundary lines, then we could lay it down or correct it. But I don't regret it. How else are we going to learn? Do we think we are so smart that we can learn something without making mistakes?

It didn't bother John to have to correct the movement and to remind us of who we are, and what God has given the Vineyard to say and do and be. I loved the whole ride! Sure, some of the time I was scared and gritting my teeth, but John wasn't and I am so glad I got to go along.

Pretentiousness

Another High Place was the Hype – the Theatrics and the Pretentiousness of so much of what purports to be the Church of Jesus Christ. He simply would not have anything to do with all that. He took the message of Jesus right off the stage, out of the four walls and he made us take it to the streets. That is what he meant when he said, 'The meat is in the street!' If anyone complained, 'Oh, I am tired of hearing the same messages – just the Milk of the Word. I want to go somewhere and get the Meat of the Word,' John would say, 'The meat is in the street – go out and do it!'

He had no greater delight than to come upon people in a shopping mall or a grocery store or in an office praying for someone. He loved it when a person was healed out in the parking lot, or had the gospel preached to them in a doctor's waiting room. He loved it when a demon was cast out in a restaurant. He didn't mind the big scene and the mess – he loved it! He'd just get that big ol' smile on his face. It never scared him to hear the screaming and shouting because he knew that person was just moments away from being set free of something that he had wanted to be free of for years. He loved it when the church broke through the walls.

Monopoly of the Ministry

Another High Place he tore down and ended, in our circle at least, was the monopoly of the ministry of the Holy Spirit by the pastor, priest, leader or the 'Star' up on the stage. 'Everybody gets to play,' he used to say. '*Everybody* gets to play!'

To prove the point once at some conference, in front of a group of academics who were frantically writing notes, he stopped and said, 'You don't get it, do you?' Looking down he saw some children and called them up to him. There was a crippled man there and John said to the children, 'You pray for him!'

'Pray for him?' they said, 'What do we say?' John answered: 'Just ask Jesus to do what you think needs to be done.' So the little boys said, 'Jesus, heal this man's broken legs!' The man was healed right then and there!

With that single event God taught the academics something that would have taken them years to understand with all their wisdom and scholarship. The ministry of the Holy Spirit is for everyone, man, woman and child: any Christian who is willing to take the risk and put their hand to whatever they sense Jesus is doing. John was always looking for what Jesus was doing. That was the guideline he went by. He never tried to make anything happen; he just kept looking to see what Jesus was doing and then he put his hand to that (John 5:19). And that is what he encouraged us all to do.

We all had a part to play in the ministry of the Holy Spirit – a ministry that for years, it seemed, had been reserved for the 'Holy Men'.

At the beginning the anointing, the power of the Holy Spirit for ministry, only came on him. It was not a group outpouring, you know. Not at the beginning. It was only John. Everybody he touched at Bible study got healed! I mean, Gigi's leg grew out an inch and a half, and when she went home that night she had to lengthen all her Levis and her mother got saved because of it!

But as wonderful as that was, the anointing still came

only on John. He was troubled because people were lining up for him to pray for them. That was not at all the way he understood it should be, and he kept reading those verses in Ephesians over and over again. 'For the equipping of the saints for the service of ministry.'

So one night at church, in the gymnasium, he called everyone forward after reading from Exodus about the consecration of the priests for ministry, how they took blood and then the oil and anointed the ear lobe, the right ear, the thumb of the right hand, the big toe of the right foot. The blood for consecration, the oil for ministry. So he called all of us up and anointed us with the oil. It was really quite moving and we understood from this that the ministry was for all of us! It was wonderful – immediately we ministered with power and confidence.

John wouldn't grasp to himself the ministry of the Holy Spirit. Everything God gave him he gave way.

Actually, he read the wrong scripture that night. Although exactly the same, he read Leviticus 14:28 instead of Exodus 29:20–21 – for the healing of infectious skin diseases. And God anointed us with the power for ministry anyway! It was hilarious!

False Piety

Another High Place was that of False Piety. He wouldn't have any of it. He wouldn't let anybody crown him king, or put robes on him or call him an apostle – (not that he ever put down the groups that had that kind of structure). When asked how he should be addressed, he said 'Just call me John.'

Once I tentatively asked him, 'Well, hey John, do you think maybe you *are* an apostle?' He answered, 'Good Grief, Carol, Nicholas Ben Gu planted thousands of churches!' (in Africa, I think) 'If there is such a thing as an apostle walking around today it is someone like him!' John was sort of impatient with that kind of speculation, not irritated exactly, but definitely impatient. 'I'm just a fat man on my way to heaven!'

There was one time though, early on, when John tried to get 'Holy', and he tried real hard. He told me one morning, in deep solemn tones, 'Carol, I am going up to the mountains to cloister myself away and I am going to fast and pray and seek the Lord's direction for the future. I don't know how many days or weeks before I shall return.' So I guess he drove up to the mountains. But about ten o'clock that night the phone rang and it was John. He said he couldn't find a room anywhere in the mountains, and he was down in San Bernadino at McDonald's eating Big Macs. I could tell he was very disappointed in himself. It was so funny and I told him to come on home and get in his warm bed, he could try some other time for the higher life.

In fact, he did learn to fast though it was never his favourite thing, and he prayed all the time, like a man talking to his friend.

Refused to Exploit People

It was important to him that people be treated with respect and allowed some dignity. He refused to exploit the vulnerability of people that is caused when the presence of God is manifest. He would never use emotion to stir people up. Those of you who have been to the conferences, do you remember how during some of the most intense times, with the excitement building higher and higher and God's presence so heavy you could hardly stand, he would stop everything for a coffee break? Then when they all came back, still chewing their cookies, he would quietly say, 'Come, Holy Spirit.' And God would break loose. Remember? It was wonderful, wasn't it? No music . . . cold turkey.

Again he would insist, 'You don't *use* worship for anything other than to worship God, and you don't use emotion either. People are emotional, and that's fine, but you don't use any thing to *cause* the ministry of the Holy Spirit. You let God be God and He will do what He will and He doesn't need "creaturely activity" (as the Quakers used to call it) to accomplish that.'

Carol Wimber's Tribute at John's Memorial Service

Worship

Which brings me to the last thing. He taught us that worship is not a vehicle to warm up the congregation for the preacher, or to soften people up for the offering. Worship comes from Jesus and goes back to Jesus from us. Everything, He gives to us, but worship belongs to Him.

We do not make stars of the worship leaders. Worship is not for any other purpose, but just for Him. That is what *He* gets. Worship is never to be used or exploited. Jesus gives everything else to us, and what He gets back from us is our worship. John taught us that . . . that was John.

There are so many things I could say about John, but as it says in 2 Kings 2:20: 'Now the rest of the acts of Hezekiah and all his might and how he made the *pool* and the *conduit* and brought *water* into the city: are they not written in the Book of the Chronicles of the Kings of Judah?'

Thank you all for coming. It blesses me that you would show that respect to him . . . because he didn't always get a lot of respect. Todd Hunter mentioned earlier in the evening that John had the hide of a rhinoceros. Well, I was reading his Bible last night and I saw what he underlined and I know that he didn't! He just put up with it because he knew it was part of it. I respected him always for keeping on and on even when his heart and body were breaking. I respected that man. It was a privilege to be his wife. God bless you all.